End

If you're tired of being triggered by past pains and allowing old wounds to limit your peace for today, read this book. Julie provides a safe place for you to be real for a moment, and she'll sit with you as you evaluate some of the painful moments in your life. Even more powerful—she gently walks you forward toward freedom from a place of knowing, care, and wisdom gained from her own experience with forgiveness. There is a kindness here, a "give it to you straight" candor, and practical memorable guides that will help you start to see your life differently: through the lens of hope, light, freedom, and fullness.

—Bethany Straarup, Associate Pastor at Elevation Church in Greensboro

This book is not merely a theoretical review of pain and forgiveness. Julie writes from a deep well of personal experience. This book is a field guide for navigating through the pain and hurt that life can throw at you. Through her own story, and a helpful set of illustrative tools, Julie will help you move toward freedom from the tyranny of unforgiveness. This book will guide you in taking practical steps—experience deep and restorative healing from emotional pain and trauma. Join Julie and make the healthy shift from despair to hope, from darkness to light, and from brokenness to breakthrough.

—Matthew Hartsfield, Lead Pastor
Bay Hope Church

Undeserved is simple, straightforward, and to the point. In an engaging and down-to-earth style, Julie Giles declares that nothing deadens the soul or inhibits spiritual growth and freedom more than refusing to forgive the unforgivable. Drawing from personal experience, she offers great inspiration and motivation to receive and give the gift of forgiveness.

—Fil Anderson, author of *Running on Empty*

I had the privilege of working with Julie Giles. She's the real deal. Watching her with small children all the way up to the elderly, the theme of her life was and is to extend reckless grace and love to those with deep hurts, habits, and hangups. Honestly? The world is in for a huge surprise because in this book Julie downloads the secrets of her heart for all of us to be inspired by and acted upon. Buckle in. You—and those you bump into—will never be the same.

—Gil Brody Jones, Spiritual Transformation
Speaker/Coach/Educator
Healing Solutions

undeserved

forgiving the unforgivable

JULIE GILES

First Paperback Edition

Some names, businesses, places, events, locales, incidents, and identifying details inside this book have been changed to protect the privacy of individuals.

Published by Freiling Publishing,
a division of Freiling Agency, LLC.

P.O. Box 1264,
Warrenton, VA 20188

www.FreilingPublishing.com

ISBN: 978-1-950948-90-1

Printed in the United States of America

dedication

Sarah, You inspired me to write! His High Places changed my life!

Isaac, You have lived this journey with me. You are my rock. SHMILY!

Heather, Jessica, Liz, Tracy, Meredith, Lori, Sandy, Janet, Cindy, Denise, Marcia, Jennifer, Josh, Jonathan, Mom. You are my village!

table of contents

preface

"A journey of a thousand miles begins with one step."
—Lao Tzu

NO PAIN EXPERIENCE should ever be wasted. On the other side, often far down the road, lessons are learned, growth is achieved, and change is created, all because an uncomfortable or downright awful situation has occurred.

Dysfunction happens when a person processes an experience and doesn't understand the correct way to store painful memories. Patterns in life are formed every single day, and when they are interrupted with dysfunctional processing, they set a wheel of events into motion that is quite hard to control. The result is chaotic living that streams through multiple settings and challenges every relationship.

There are people in your life who have hurt you, some more than others, and you are walking around carrying weight placed on your shoulders from that relationship.

We carry shame, hurt, resentment, anger, and other powerful emotions inside of relational pain. Carry those feelings long enough and they will change who you are, sometimes for good, and sometimes not. The individual who has hurt you the most may not even be aware of the pain they have inflicted, yet you allow them to hurt you by carrying grudges, disappointment, or regret.

If you had the power to cut all of that loose, to let go of it for today and for always, would you do it? Of course, you would! In fact, you possess a picture in your mind of what it would be like to be free from their influence. Even if it was something tiny, you don't want others to have power over you.

Life is lived moment by moment, and each day you are on planet Earth you have made choices that add up to become who you are today. If you are a living, breathing human, you have done some things you are very proud of and others that you are not. You have experienced running away and lunging forward. You have dug up some things that should have been left alone and buried things that should have been treasured. Who you are has been defined in the actions you have taken.

Who you are today has been created in incremental steps. You have grown in tiny moments and great moments, and you have failed in small experiences as well as great ones. I'm here to tell you that you are more than the sum of your failures, and so are the people you have encountered in life. Freedom is found when we choose to lay aside what we deserve, pick up the pieces, and move forward.

The word "deserve" has a lot of meaning. It is often seen as a negative term. We often get things we don't deserve. If I win a million dollars, that is probably not because I earned it. If you don't like a consequence, like a traffic ticket, you might see it as undeserved. A child deserves punishment when they disobey. A criminal deserves a consequence when they commit a crime. If you were to think of the things in life you deserve that you haven't gotten, are they causing you to look into the rearview mirror with anger, frustration, or ill thoughts? Has someone withheld something you felt you deserved?

I've spoken to adults who didn't get something as a child, and the memory is still carried into adulthood. I've met people whose feelings were hurt in their teens, and in their fifties they still remember like it was yesterday. Each of us carries memories that rob us of peaceful living. And each of us needs to make the choice to let go of the grip they have on us. But that is not as easy, and you know it.

The great news is there is hope for your future. You can stop allowing the things you've carried around to influence you.

Today is a new day. With the proper attention, you have the power to leave the past behind. The potential is here to uncover a future filled with healthy living, encouraging words, and possibilities like you have not allowed yourself to encounter for a long time. YOU are in for the most transformative journey of your life, and we will get there together.

So who am I? First, I am your cheerleader, a fellow pain carrier, and a first-hand trauma expert. My name is Julie, and my story has led me to a place where I found darkness in every corner, pain in every crevice, and light at the end of the tunnel. My passion has always been to help others. My journey has brought me from the bottom to the top, and I am optimistic yours will too.

Pain has a way of lingering longer than it should, and I've experienced the liberating freedom of letting it go. I found that freedom in the most unexpected place—forgiveness. In this practice, you too can discover that life can be more than just existing each day. Bringing back the person you ought to be, want to be, or forgot you were is more than possible, and when you do, your future will be rescripted. I believe that you will find tools inside this care package that took me years to discover.

So who are you? My fellow wounded heart. You are a fragile person, a person of worth, an incredible individual whose life has meaning. You might even be someone with a container of pain pushed down and packed inside, and you may be living in a land of devastation. You're likely juggling a massive stack of messy life experiences waiting to be dropped all over the floor. You are an individual who wants to share honestly and desires freedom. You are you, and you are essential, and you are what makes this process worthwhile. You are *valuable!*

There is a third individual in this experience, and that is God. His desire is for you to be whole, to be healthy, and to be the best version of yourself possible. He made you, He loves you, and He wants to see you thrive. Not only is He a part of our experience, but He is also the author of forgiveness. His life has shown us that grace is the element necessary for letting go of the past. His life's mission was based on our need to experience forgiveness, and in His example of grace-filled living, we can give forgiveness to others—even when it is undeserved. As you read these pages, I would encourage you to stop and consider God's role in your success plan. Talk with

Him openly and consider His perspective as you contemplate each question.

Your experience with God as we work together will be different from others, but there will be similarities as well. I invite you to find someone else to share your thoughts with. There is healing inside a conversation, and finding a friend to be open and honest with will allow you to have a more profound experience. If this is the first time you've considered God's influence in your life, that's okay too. There is room for all types of individuals at this table, and rest assured, no one is perfect or judging your thoughts and ideas.

Crisis has a way of presenting itself differently to each of us. The same crisis can have different effects on you than it has on anyone else. Sometimes you will handle a problem like a heavyweight champion, and other times you feel like you've lost an unwinnable war. Your heart may be heavy as we speak, or you may be in a great place. No matter where you are, our time together will help you prepare for the next time you are faced with a life-altering blow.

The journey ahead is about being an overcomer enabled to face obstacles like fear, shame, anger, resentment, and abandonment. You will be given an opportunity to grieve the past and actively live in the present. This isn't a magical potion or a book with step-by-step answers. It's more like a friend walking with you down a dark and lonely path. We're walking away from painful experiences, setting aside deep hurt, and we are discovering healing for wounds of every shape and size. Look down the road; a bright light is in the distance, and in the light, warmth and beauty are overflowing. It's growing more prominent, and you're getting closer. That light, my friend, is the natural function of forgiveness.

I would strongly urge you to pick up a journal and write your thoughts as we move along. The pace is yours to set.

Note: The following few pages contain mention of events that may disturb or land close to home for some—don't let that stop you from reading as my wounds are part of my story and my success.

my dysfunction story

THOUGH I'VE HAD incredible opportunities in life, I've struggled to feel connected and completely whole. My life has been filled with insufficient processing of memories and decisions to allow others to control my destiny. Inside the messiness, I have gained firsthand knowledge of struggle and deep wounds that have changed my life forever. I have also had to figure out a way to stop hiding all of the layers of dysfunction I was carrying. Packed up like a heavy suitcase ready to explode, I drug my pain around as if I were responsible for keeping it alive.

One hundred percent of the people on this planet have experienced pain. Some have experienced trauma. And some have endured the unthinkable. But all of us have a choice to make. We can let it control us, or we need to let go of it to gain the upper hand. This journey should not be done alone. I wonder where God fits into this equation for you. Each step you take can be done on your own, but the possibilities are miraculously multiplied when you allow God to join you along the way. When you let go of pain, you can then grasp onto the future with both hands. Embracing the possibilities means letting God have control. When we talk about the word "forgiveness," sometimes the place we have to start is with our faith. I challenge you to open your heart to the possibility that God needs to be invited to join you as we move forward.

Though the journey ahead is uniquely yours, *you and I* have similarities. No person on the planet has everything figured out, and none of us has handled every situation exactly as we should. Like me, you have people in your life that need your forgiveness. Some of them deserve it, and others don't. Some of them are stuck in their own journey waiting for yours to change. My story involves a few people who needed my forgiveness but had no right to ask for it. Sometimes I still find myself taking a deep breath when I think backward in time, and

I hear small, whispering voices that remind me of where I have come from.

I hate secrets. I don't like to keep them, and I don't like to ask others to keep them either. That's partly because I am incredibly curious and partly because I'm a problem solver. My childhood was filled with dirty little secrets tucked neatly away from the surface, and my childhood was a maze of opportunities to solve the problems with which I was presented.

My parents fell in love at a young age, and though they came from different sides of the social spectrum, they got married and had three children. I was in the middle. But don't be deceived by picket fences or church attendance; our family was far from perfect. I grew up believing that every family has secrets that are better kept locked away. Today I work very hard to find common ground with my mom, and I'm happy to report that we have each extended grace across the barriers; our healing journey is well underway. But this story took a lot of twists and turns before we got to that point.

In the fall of 1970, after a long and difficult pregnancy, I was born—four weeks late. From the very start, my mom and I struggled with bonding, and that lack of connection presented many struggles for me throughout the years—mostly because I just wanted to be wanted, and yet neither of us knew how to go back and fix that.

My dad grew up in a strict home with a lot of instability. We heard stories of food insecurity and frequent movement around the country. Education was not nearly the priority it should have been. After years of blue-collar work, he finished his college education at age 34.

Most of my early memories involve my father's harsh responses to my behavior. He was a strong man who knew that children needed guidance and direction, but he, like many men in his generation, missed the need for nurture and understanding. He was the bearer of a strong arm and a belt. I can appreciate his desire to raise a family of well-behaved, intelligent decision-makers that worked hard. Still, his strict rules and high expectations left an enormous amount of fear in my heart that I would give anything to remove.

At times my older brother was my curiosity companion, my friend, and my creative thought processor, but the same firm hand that jolted my world was present in his. We loved our dad, but we never knew exactly what to expect from him. I don't remember how old we were the first time we plotted to run away, but those conversations happened often.

In elementary school, I observed my brother's actions, including destroying small animals, insects, and inanimate objects. I listened to him plot bizarre traps and plan torture devices. In time, I was the test subject for his schemes.

Before I even became a teenager, I was sexually abused by more than one person for an extended period of time. With each violation, I was introduced to feelings of shame, inadequacy, and tangled emotions. Most teens struggle with insecurity and identity, but I was confused by continuously mixed messages. Betrayal, fear, intimidation, and bewilderment were among the lies that created an avalanche of emotions in my life.

Before you think this house was out of control and couldn't have been worse, let me tell you the good things. We had three meals a day, a dog and a cat, and various other animals like horses. We had consistent education, and we appeared to be "the normal family." We attended church, had a clean house, and ate dinner together. People actually wanted to be like us—though I'm confident they had no idea what they wished. We went on vacations and took Sunday drives; we had people over for dinner and had what we needed. It wasn't on the surface where things were wrong.

At age 17, I left home, and I found my voice. It was a mess, and I had no idea how to make it work, but I found it. While the shy country girl, intimidated and knocked down, became sassy and outspoken, new challenges emerged on the scene. Unfortunately, the cost of those years of negative feedback lingered in my identity. I could speak loudly, but I didn't understand my own emotions. Each relationship I had left me with more questions than answers. Was this love? Was this belonging? Was this pain, rejection, abandonment? Would he love me unconditionally? Would he hurt me?

The biggest problem was that I had no idea how the rest of the world managed these feelings. I had never seen them modeled in a way I understood. Most significantly, I had no idea how deeply my wounds were embedded or why they couldn't be washed away.

I read books, burned friendships, studied others' behaviors, blew up romantic relationships, watched videos, went to counseling, and still sabotaged some of the best connections I could have made. In my active quest to survive, I had forgotten to give myself any grace. Before long, I was right in the middle of my dysfunctional mess. I was writing new chapters of my life, and they were a train wreck.

Like building armor for my future self, I found tools that were more destructive than helpful. I learned to replace my shortcomings with perfectionism nurtured by how I allowed unrealistic expectations to be created by just about everyone in my life.

I wish my pain and my dysfunction ended with these lifelong contributors. Others hurt me throughout the years—the school bully, groups of unkind church ladies, and the coworkers that gossiped when my brother's prison sentence was announced. Taking a closer look, I realized the most significant contributor to this dysfunction was my decision to carry baggage from one broken experience to the next. Each one contributed to further pain, and getting rid of the initial problem would have prevented residual incidents. At the time it became apparent that I needed to move on, but to do that I had to offer forgiveness to myself and to others that had created elements of my chaotic living. When I pause to assess the rearview mirror, I am intrigued. I found giving forgiveness to people outside my family was pretty easy. After all, they never made it physical or knew the whole story. I had amassed a pretty good set of avoidance tactics, and they worked well, keeping my dysfunction at arm's length.

The day arrived when I was confronted by a life-altering question: "Why do we need forgiveness anyway?" Some well-meaning people would tell you just to move on and not worry about forgiving people in your past. And for the ease of moving forward, that might make sense. But at a certain point in life, those past experiences will revisit you in an unsettling way. For Christians, "There is a connection between what God does and what you do. You can't get forgiveness from God, for instance, without also forgiving others. If you refuse to do your part, you cut yourself off from God's part (Matthew 6:14-15, MSG). Forgiveness is such an important ingredient of truly experiencing freedom from the past, and I believe it is the single most important element of this conversation.

Sadly, I had developed an avoidance strategy that allowed me to ignore the shortcomings of others and believe I had forgiven them. I knew if I tried my usual tools, I could prove to unkind people that they should like me. And in my need to be accepted, that tactic felt pretty good. I became an overachiever so that people wouldn't think of me as damaged goods. I could outwork them, out commit, outgive, out _____ (fill in the blank) them. You name it, and I was pretty good at most of it.

But proving that I was worthy of love and acceptance always fell apart somewhere down the line.

I studied life, I practiced giving, and I tried to feel normal. If I could just dig deep enough, I could press through. I became exceptionally good at the survival game. The good news is, I found help. I allowed people to walk with me through true forgiveness and actually understand why my broken heart kept cycling through the breaking process. And I discovered that Jesus cared about my pain. Not only did He care, but He also wanted me to find freedom from its influence. Some journeys of forgiveness are short and straightforward, while others take more time and perseverance.

I was on a quest to get rid of the past and move forward, and I was going to do it by conquering the world and protecting my younger sister. I committed to a life of surviving, but I dreamed of a life of thriving and tried multiple avenues in search of healing. I had gotten pretty good at appearing to thrive when I was busy, committed, and making other people happy. But when things calmed down, I felt empty, and my heart ached for resolution. But I still felt an empty ache inside.

I began pushing back. My rebellion got me in a lot of trouble, but it also gave me the strength to change. I love that my story is about a woman that pressed against the odds, grew up, had a beautiful family, experienced a wonderful marriage, and loved her career. I could check the boxes of success. Graduate school—check; beautiful home—check; great friends—check; the list goes on. But my story is incomplete without the recognition of my faith. At first, it gave me courage. In time, it gave me strength, and as I began to surrender, it gave me healing.

Here are five dysfunctions I learned because I didn't know how to manage my pain. Each of these has led to a portion of this book.

1. What others do: Talk about it. What I did: I had no idea how to talk about anything. Every conversation led to a need to be heard more than a need to connect. I was fighting the fear of abandonment, and my friends didn't even know they had the opportunity to abandon me.

2. What others do: Negotiate. What I did: I had learned to give others anything they wanted. I had no idea how to get what I wanted or even what I needed. My means for negotiation was agreement. If you wanted something from me, I agreed—you could have it. I hoped by making others happy, somehow I would find my happiness. One thing I knew: if I gave happiness away, I wouldn't be taking it away.

3. What others do: Stick with it. What I did: I had no idea how to see something through to the end. I'm observant. Really observant. I notice if you are doing something wrong, I notice if someone else thinks I have done something wrong, and I follow the rules to avoid shame. I could finish a task and end well, but shame was the emotion that ruled my mind if someone didn't like it.

4. What others do: Listen. What I did: I had to learn to hear others. Not everyone who criticizes does it with bad intentions. I took every piece of negative feedback personally. I've had to learn to listen to people's suggestions as helpful. I'm on a constant quest for affirmation. It's not an affirmation that you like me; it's the affirmation that I've done what you expect. It's a way of staying ahead of the anger curve. I will test people's relationships. Sometimes I don't even know that I'm doing it.

5. What others do: Stay. What I did: If put in the right setting, I will do absolutely anything to keep someone from getting angry at me. I would leave, hide, lie, trade favors, or manipulate to keep the anger out of your response settings. I had a fear of anger more than a fear of death. I had to learn to stay and face an individual to manage how we could interact in the future.

I've had to learn my "tell signs" to face my struggle and embrace discomfort. If I neglect any one of these, it's possible to slip back into the destructive habits of people pleasing and self-sabotage. Below are five questions that helped me know when I am looking at things from the wrong perspective. When I hear myself asking them, I know it's time to reframe the questions.

1. How do I earn your approval? When I hear that question, my mind recognizes it and changes to, *How can I help you succeed?* Thus taking away the ability for others to manipulate me.

2. Do I deserve your affection? This question comes from a head voice shouting: *Am I worthy of good things in my life?* It says, *Your affection would be wonderful, but I don't have to prove it to you. I hope you notice my efforts, but if you don't, my identity is not wrapped up in the decision you have made.*

3. Am I worthy of love? This is another question that leans toward identity. Of course, I'm worthy of love, but acceptance is at the heart of what I'm looking for. I hope you don't abandon me, and you can show me that you will instead love me unconditionally, even when I don't deserve it. I'll promise to do the same for you. "How can we better connect?" is my new and improved question.

4. What do I need to do to keep your approval? This is a lie in and of itself. If my actions are required for your happiness, something is wrong. I don't have to earn your approval, and you don't have permission to destroy me when you disapprove. The better question should be, "I would like to do something meaningful. What would be the most significant thing I could do for you right now?"

5. What did I do to deserve this treatment? Of course you don't deserve abuse, mistreatment, alienation, or abandonment. The real question is, do I need to stay in a relationship with this person who is treating me this way? I'd like to answer that for you—the answer is no. And that's so much easier to say to you than it is to live for me. I'm sure you will find the same challenge.

The most beautiful piece of my story is the realization that God carried me each step of the way, and even in the worst moments, He was there as my comfort, my strength, and my shield. We could focus on my life story, dysfunction, or shortcomings, but this story is about you. Where do you need to change your habits? What people do you need to move far away from? Whose influence is destroying your life? Who has been permitted to betray your connections?

It's my prayer that you will see how easily these patterns destroy, and you will either stop inflicting them upon others or stop allowing them to be imposed upon you. When I was younger, I learned that love must be earned, that achievement was worth more than grace, and that my identity was wrapped up in other people's opinions. I was wrong, but I couldn't fix them until I started with forgiveness.

Are you ready to start in the right place? It's going to take work, and the honest answers may not be what you want to hear. A transformation will be needed in your heart and mind and even the steps you take. One thing I do know: if I can do it, you can do it. I'm here and committed to the journey. Get your shoes; we've got a long walk ahead.

1

the starting line

"Where the heart is willing, it will find a thousand ways. Where it is unwilling, it will find a thousand excuses."
—Arlen Price

CONGRATULATIONS! BY OPENING this book, you have just taken the first step of an essential journey that will change your life. Think of it like a race and you are just lining up at the starting block.

Take a deep breath and keep your heart and mind open. It's time to head for the finish line, but to win, you have to run the race. That means you've got to participate in the process.

I decided to return to school in my forties, adding a few degrees to my higher education portfolio. Today I am a few steps away from obtaining a PhD. Education has served me well, but relationships are the essence of everything that matters. Bad relationships have taught me just as much as good ones, and good ones have proven much harder to maintain.

Influencers have made me strong, bold, courageous, broken, wounded, and even utterly helpless at times. If it is true that relationships are what make life have a purpose, we must uncover what makes us resort to lonely rituals when our relationships fail.

I've always been a planner, an analyzer, and a problem solver. I can clearly see the result before we even begin. What is life without a plan for the future? Can you identify?

What do the voices in your head say? You know the ones; they sneer with unkindness or clamor like a noisy gong, delivering convoluted tunes to your soul. Wounds appear to soak up their melody and nurture heartbreak and frustration.

Life's journey has a way of creating tangled webs that demand focus. Not everything you uncover will be bad. By looking carefully enough, you'll discover evidence of things that are not actually broken at all. They hide in plain sight, and they hide in the darkest corners. Today I want to share the gift of finding something broken, recognizing it, and setting it back into place.

You can say many things about me, but a morning person is not one of them. I would be happy never to experience life before 10:00 a.m., and noon would be even better. But the rest of the world doesn't work that way, so I've learned that I have to adjust. It's painful at times and a real struggle nearly every time the alarm sounds. Even worse than getting up tired is that feeling that I have unfinished business to complete. I try never to go to bed with a project undone. My first instinct is to procrastinate things that were left unfinished when I went to bed, and procrastination turns to dread when I have to face what was left undone.

You may be the opposite. You may be a morning person, and you will put a big project off until you're fresh in the early hours of the day. Regardless of when you are at your peak performance, you share my dread for things left undone. It's something we share across race, religion, gender, and even cultural lines. Facing the inevitable is something that has to happen eventually unless you can manage to ignore it, to run from it, to hide it, or to give it away.

When you consider your past, what would you say is your most common mode of dealing with complex issues? Do you tuck them away for another day, or do you face them head-on? Most of us are afraid of things we aren't in control of, and we tend to let them steal our energy by haunting our thoughts and overwhelming our schedule. That project you need to finish sits in the corner, not because you have forgotten about it, but because you fear finishing it wrong. You worry that you won't have the energy to get it done to the level of satisfaction you desire or because you have created an excuse that will contradict itself.

The brokenness of the world we live in magnifies our excuse making. Dysfunction occurs when we move about without facing reality. We avoid our own inability to achieve the results we desire, perpetuating the procrastination well beyond a reasonable timeline. Few people have absolutely no problem with procrastination, which helps us understand one another's tactics with compassion.

My procrastination happens in pockets. Some tasks go straight into the "do it later" pile. I hate to file. I put files into baskets. Essential papers in one, legal documents in one, and things I need to pay attention to very soon in the third. A file cabinet sits in the corner, but I rarely open it. Putting things into folders, labeling and alphabetizing them, and remembering what folder they went into is a daunting task. I could do the job well, but it would take more time than it's worth if I did. So instead I have cheated the system with my baskets. Last year I even bought bigger baskets so I wouldn't have to open the dreaded drawers. Just how long do you need to keep tax returns anyway?

Do you use this method in dealing with daily life? Do you compartmentalize things you like, things you don't like, and things you completely dread? Do you gloss over your inaction by creating dysfunctional systems to deal with the negligent decisions you've made? Do you explain away dysfunctional habits because they make sense in your own mind?

Several years ago I realized I had begun using this method to deal with pain and trauma in my life. That was a bad idea. I dealt with easy things. I took them head-on. I spoke to people who would understand they had hurt my feelings. But other people got put into the procrastination box. They might be dealt with later—if I ever got to them. And if they moved away or left the company before we had necessary conversations, I won—I had avoided the conflict altogether. You're probably reading this realizing just how bad this habit was, but I was living it and couldn't see the forest for the trees. I needed to fix the dysfunction.

When I got even more serious about the procrastination of conflict, pain in my life, and profoundly seeded woundedness, I realized the compartments had a very dark side. I had locked some of the pain and trauma so far away that I believed it was dealt with. But things tucked away tend to bubble up to the surface at the most inopportune times. They show up when we least expect, and they have a way of spoiling everything they touch.

My own journey included a path of hidden trauma mixed with compartmentalized dysfunction, and when I finally faced it head-on, I realized there was a theme running through every instance of pain I had buried. I had not dealt with the source of circumstances that had wounded me. This was true in small things and big things. Not only had I not dealt with those things, but I had also not dealt with the people who were involved.

A straightforward word connected all of the pain in my life, and I have to tell you, it's not the word I wanted it to be. It was much easier to believe I was above all of those problems. I would love to say that I didn't have a part to play. I would have been relieved to know that it was someone else's fault. But dragging all of that around for so many years was unhealthy. At times it was debilitating. And at times the pain created even more pain. The cycle was one I wished to end, but I had to figure out the key. So what's the word? Unforgiveness.

Yuck! That word sounds awful! And as I say it aloud, I'm embarrassed by its implications. Is it possible that my unwillingness to let go of the past is tied up in my reluctance to resolve forgiveness issues? I would prefer to hide this conversation in its own dedicated file box and never return to it. But the dysfunction that drives me to this desire is the reason I need to deal with it. This means I need to own it, to face it, and to unbury it.

You've picked up this book because you have relationships with other people, and there is strain, tension, or brokenness blocking your view of the future. But that doesn't mean it has to stay that way. There is significance in what your mind is processing right now. I want to be sure you keep that significance in mind as we move forward. Your job is to simply keep moving forward, even when you want to quit. This journey is worth walking—I promise.

There's good news for you, dear reader. I see potential in you and in your journey, and I want you to be able to see it too. You are not destined for unending loneliness or dysfunction that lasts forever. Every connection you have illuminates the spotlight of truth. And the truth is that your life matters and your relationships define just how much.

2

the gift

"If you, God, kept records on wrongdoings, who would stand a chance? As it turns out, forgiveness is your habit, and that's why you're worshiped" (Psalm 130:3, MSG).

ARE YOU A one-trip wonder? You know, the person who unpacks everything in the car on a single trip? Do you carry all of it, no matter how strenuous the job becomes? I've found myself juggling a cell phone, laptop, groceries, car seats, keys, coffee, mail … just because I thought I must make it in a single trip, believing that coming back to the car would be too much trouble.

Many of us carry life the same way. We pack everything possible into a single minute, overload ourselves with stress, or haul all of our past negativity around. We add each memory on top of the last until the weight is too much to manage. Offloading those experiences seems nearly impossible without knocking us off-balance.

In the cartoons, animators draw the familiar scene that seems funny to watch but less fun to experience. They poke fun as viewers wait for just the right moment. The character with arms filled to overflowing balances their load and attempts to move forward, suddenly they trip, and we laugh as everything goes flying out of control. Sound effects emphasize the disastrous moment, and the bump on top of the head grows out of control.

Have you picked up unnecessary messages that make you believe there is a need to carry all that weight alone? What if you don't? Would there be devastating consequences?

Take a seat and think about all that is in your hands today. Ask yourself if you need to carry it all. Let me help you understand what I mean. First, let's acknowledge that you have a purpose in life. And let's acknowledge that others sometimes have the ability to knock that purpose right out from under you. And let's agree that life would be better if you could frame that purpose well. And together, let's agree that living outside of your purpose can be problematic. As we begin to work together, I've prepared an imaginary package for you. It's a gift. It's not another weight to carry; in fact, it will relieve some of the things piling up in your life right now. I'm giving it to you. It's yours to keep (forever).

Right this moment I'm extending your official invitation. Sitting before you is your figurative gift box. Imagine it with a giant red bow on top; it's heavy and waiting. You need to know that it comes with strings attached. They are connected to every person you have and ever will meet. You may not need to forgive them all, but the conversation in this book can be applied when and where you need it most. When you're ready, take a breath … and open the box.

The package in your hands contains a deep and meaningful experience. Let's start by reading the not-so-imaginary card.

Dear ____________ (that's you),

Today is a new day. Let's seize the moment and commit to a few things.

First, let's commit to hard work and perseverance. Second, let's commit to sticking together—I'm here to support you. It's going to take an effort and willingness to be painfully honest with yourself to move forward. And finally, let's work hard to redefine my life's purpose as God intended it to be. It will be worth it.

You've got this!

From: ______________ (that's you too)

I love to get mail. Well, not junk mail, but the good stuff. You know, cards, especially with money inside. Cheesy pictures or sappy sayings don't remove the beauty of a well-timed envelope and matching stationery. Texts, email, snail mail, or hand-scribbled notes that hold a perfectly timed message can brighten any day. But not every message is a treasure. The power of a terrible message can linger like a ghost. These words taunt you in moments of insecurity.

Insecurity happens when we have placed value on the wrong things. When we devalue God's plan for our own life, we are left with a giant hole inside that aches to be filled. The great news is, God is here to set that straight. When you place your identity in Him, you will see your insecurity reduced.

Has anyone ever screamed, "You don't belong here!" right in your face? In my case, they weren't said in a hate-filled, angry tone; they were made as a statement as the individual walked out of the room. Those exact words were spoken to me by a coworker. I was stunned, but I didn't know what to do with them. Instead of processing through their painful teeth, I just let them sit, and brew, and fester, and ferment, and build up inside of me. I still didn't know how to handle them, but I had let them steal my joy. Not only that, but they also made me self-conscious, hurt, and feel unwanted. I could have carried that around for the rest of my life, but I decided to do something about it. I faced it—head-on—and I'm here to tell you that facing hard things is hard, but not meeting them is even more complicated. No matter how old you are, words can hurt you. And the words she said that day were mean-spirited, but I had to learn to deal with them healthily.

Thinking about that experience reminds me of a terrible day when I was six years old. Our pony was pretty and standing in the field, so I decided to ride her. Just a few minutes later, I was sitting on the ground in a big patch of cactus. Hundreds, maybe thousands of prickly pear needles had pierced my skin. Each one needed to be carefully removed, and each of them hurt more coming out than going in. But collectively they had the power to debilitate me if they were not released.

Cactus in my legs, arms, back, and feet were nothing compared to many of the other painful experiences I've had in my life. Still, I understand today that the process for dealing with pain is similar, no matter how big or small the situation. Left unattended, pain can lead to dysfunction, or dealt with properly can lead to personal growth. I'm proud to stand today saying that my memorable cactus experience taught me a huge lesson. I could blame the pony for throwing me or blame the cactus for blooming, but if I had worn jeans and boots, the needles would have had a much more difficult time inflicting their pain.

My decision to wear shorts and flip-flops was a poor wardrobe choice, and was mine to own. I couldn't remove the damage on my own, and I learned that I had to ask for help and endure the painful process of removing each sharp point.

I wonder if you have a story like mine. Have you experienced pain that introduced you to life's lessons or pain that required you to get help to face it? Dysfunction happens in our lives when we don't end the pain, when we perpetuate the cycle, or when we stuff the pain deeper down. The answer to living freely is dealing with the results of our life experiences, whether we got ourselves into the mess or if someone else got us there through their hatefulness. Life cannot be lived to the fullest when dysfunction is present, and rarely do we walk through life making all of the best decisions day after day. That means we need help. *All of us!*

In a few weeks, months, or years I want to see you standing up, having grown through your own life experience. I want to know that you have faced tough challenges and won. I want to see you standing up and cheering for the future.

Life is filled with cactus patch moments, mean words, and much worse. My story includes lost friendships, broken relationships, sexual abuse, and more than I could ever write about. But because I have chosen to look for solutions, work the process of painful resolution, and allow God to change my heart, I stand beside you. Today is your opportunity to take the next step.

Traveling through life is like driving a car down a city street. Sometimes we encounter nothing but green lights and move effortlessly in the desired direction. But a stoplight when we're already running late can illuminate tension or frustration. Would turning left or right change the course and allow for a better journey? Do you second-guess your route, speed up, change lanes, or simply wait for the light to change?

When a roadblock happens in your daily life, do you keep moving in the same direction? Do you wonder if you're even on the right road to begin with? The easy choice is to quit—to take the road with fewer obstacles. But there is another choice. You can decide never to allow this roadblock to stop you again. It takes planning, intention, and decisions that help you get unstuck today and in the future. Look in the mirror and ask yourself this question: "Am I ready to deal with my pain and end its influence?"

Envision yourself standing on a ledge. To save yourself, you must grab a hand that is just beyond your comfort zone. Wiggling fingers motion you forward, but you can't touch them. Would you be willing to do it? Do you trust yourself enough to push off of the solid ground you're standing on? Can you take the leap? How well you trust the person on the other side of that hand determines your willingness to let go. What will go wrong if you decide to stay here, on the ledge … forever? You know that this scenario can't end well if danger is behind you. At some point you have to let go and jump with all your might. Close your eyes if you must, but do it. You have to jump!

The answer to moving forward cannot and must not be one that adds to the dysfunction. One bad set of habits can't be replaced by another one. And staying in this place is not an option either. If you are at a crossroads and considering your choices, the answer to leaving the past behind is actually present in the most unexpected place. You'll find while working through the process, you'll encounter a long list of decisions, but to completely let go of the past, you have to consider what is holding you back. What have you been dragging along with you? If you had to let go of all of the past to reach forward, could you do it?

What would tempt you to hold on? Is there one little piece you'd like to pick up and coddle? Would you find yourself nurturing your pain and having a difficult time letting go? This is the danger zone where it could unravel. Your forward momentum could be stopped. You may second-guess and wonder if you should be on a different path. Believe me; this will be the area you want to avoid, the place you create the most compelling excuses for procrastination, and the arena where you decide that going off-road will be easier than staying the course.

3

the secret place

"I have an increasing sense that the most important crisis of our time is spiritual. We need places where people can grow stronger in the spirit and be able to integrate the emotional struggles in their spiritual journeys."

—Henri Nouwen

THERE IS A place in each of us where we tuck away hurt feelings, deep wounds, and chronically painful memories. Nobody is allowed into this zone without a special invitation. You may even believe this place is so dark that God can't reach it. And sometimes when you go there your thought life becomes scrambled and you emerge anxious, depressed, angry, sad, or generally worse off than you were when you went inside. Barbed-wire emotions and caution-light conversations guard this junkyard with care. The do-not-enter sign is posted for all of your loved ones, and no one dares to enter this zone.

Resolving the baggage tucked away in this space will be more complicated than any other pain and emotion you have filed away. In order to take the leap, you'll have to leave it all behind and let go. This pain is God's, and He is willing to carry it if you let Him. Psalm 50:15 reminds us to ask Him for help when we experience trouble. That's a great place to start.

No hard thing you face should be left unnoticed. The most painful situations are the most significant. They build character. They change you and grow you into the person you need to be tomorrow and the next day. Each time you face another challenge, you win by becoming a better version of yourself.

Do you know who that person is? Who is it that you are meant to be? Are you able to envision a new version of yourself? We know that with God all things are possible—even dealing with something from the past. Of course, not all pain is the same. There are various levels of wounds you carry around. Some will be harder to let go of and others will take some time. I must tell you—it won't be easy. But I can promise you it will bring freedom, a new perspective of every relationship you have, and you will leave with a refreshed view of yourself. Step into this process boldly or with hesitation—but step—jump if you must. You can't move forward by slipping backward. And you can't make progress if you're sitting still. The only choice is forward even if you can't envision what that looks like.

When you feel helpless, stuck, hopeless, scared, hurt, worried, or anxious, allowing yourself to stay in that space is not only dysfunctional for today, but it also has ripple effects that negatively change your future. Filing your emotions into the wrong drawer is just as dangerous as sitting still at a stoplight for several rotations.

Are you ready to go? What do you need freedom from? What compartments do you need to empty and analyze? What past issues do you need to face head-on? Whatever that thing is, this book will help you move forward from your self-inflicted avoidance into a place where you can let it go and celebrate the person you are to become.

Every person on Earth has reasons why unfinished business lurks inside of their meaningful relationships. You've missed essential conversations, carried hurt feelings, experienced deep wounds, encountered heartache. You have developed a special place where you hide sensitive feelings. Some days that feels like a million pounds of pressure or emulates a feeling of total numbness. Your mind overanalyzes it and calls it regret. Do you know why?

No two people carry the same identical weight, even when associated with the same exact trauma. All of us process difficult situations, but understanding someone else's whirling emotions is like walking through a twisting, turning maze in total darkness.

Your emotions matter, and being honest with yourself as you encounter those emotions will help the journey ahead to be successful. At some point, you will come eye-to-eye with memories that need processing. They lunge at you filled with resentment, rejection, or anger, while their persistence nags at you until they are eventually resolved. Although you don't know all of the "why" answers, it is time to discover the significance of these recollections.

When you feel devalued, unloved, or misunderstood, you begin to experience regret or isolate yourself from God. In those moments when you think your opinion doesn't matter, you may create excuses to validate your feelings. You may even lie or slip back into uncomfortably destructive behavior patterns. When others remove your valid feelings, they have crossed boundaries into your life that cause regret. Over time that regret builds up like air in a balloon. Let that build long enough and it will explode.

If we could measure it, put it all in a single bucket, and discover just how full the container is, how much regret would you say is sitting inside your heart and mind today? The problem is, your brain takes messy feelings associated with devaluing moments and processes the message to make you feel manipulated, used, or unworthy. Plain and simple—you feel like a mess, and it's because of unresolved relational regret.

My question to you—how much regret are you currently holding onto? How much is too much?

Let me introduce you to a reality where this persistence can be resolved. You may already be well acquainted with resolution but seem to be stuck in one specific scenario. Your mind believes you are completely trapped and remains uncertain while you aimlessly wander around trying to reduce your Regret Influence score.

Do you wonder what your Regret Influence Score is? Let's take a quick quiz. You'll need a blank piece of paper. (A journal might be an excellent place to collect your thoughts.)

Regret Influence Assessment

- List your top ten regrets.
- You can list more, but don't get lost in the exercise.
- I recommend setting a timer. (Five minutes should do.)
- Don't discount the little ones and be sure to record the big ones.
- Now, give each a "pain present" score. 1 = just a little and 10 = unbearable.
- You can determine the numbers in between.
- Now add up your score and record your total.

Your Regret Influence score is not an exact science. It should, however, be a great indicator of things you are carrying around without resolution. Any single regret with a score of more than four indicates unresolved baggage.

A cumulative Regret Influence Score in the double digits should be eye opening. If your score has crossed the fifty points line, you are unquestionably experiencing a significant amount of debilitating pain.

4

the permission slip

Do something on this day that
your future self will thank you for.
—Unknown

NOBODY GOES THROUGH life without traumatic experiences.

- **Rule #1:** Never allow hurt feelings to resolve by simply avoiding people connected to the circumstances that brought them on.
- **Rule #2:** When it comes to habitual offenders, those who hurt you repeatedly, you absolutely must change the way your relationship functions.
- **Rule #3:** There's no one-size-fits-all resolution plan.

- **Rule #4:** Some tools are more effective than others in helping your relationships thrive. Try each one and discover when it best fits the situation.
- **Rule #5:** If you have contributed to someone else's pain (you have), contemplate your missteps and the places you might need to ask for forgiveness as well.
- **Rule #6:** God has a place in your permission journey. Be sure to include Him in the process.

Let's dive in!

Returning to the imaginary gift box that you encountered on the first pages of the book, you'll notice a string. Take it out and keep it handy.

The amount of pain we endure lands somewhere between a blip in the day and debilitating. Your body is an excellent indicator of stored-up pain, suffering, regret, and anxiety. Notice your shoulders, back, and neck; consider your irregular stomach or gained weight. Your body tells when you are holding onto the past in unhealthy ways. Before taking off the reconciliation trail, I wonder if you can identify where your body is speaking loudest. See if any surprising changes occur in the coming weeks.

The people you encounter each day need permission from you. They need permission to talk with you—you give it to them when you listen and return the conversation, when you smile at them, or when you allow their interruptions. By interacting with others, you are giving them permission. You can award them with attention, conversation, or any type of response, even if just for a moment.

Exercise #1

Let's do a little exercise in permission giving. Here is where the string comes in. Twirl it around your index finger (not too tightly). Paying close attention to the speed of your choices, read the scenario line by line. When you encounter this symbol, ‡, it's time to make a decision. If the details prompted you to say yes, signify that by unwrapping one loop from your hand. If your answer is no, do nothing. Each new line represents a new loop. Will you unwrap it, or will you keep it around your finger?

Scenario #1

It's a beautiful day and you have just parked your car at the local grocery store.

You wave to someone as you cross the parking lot.

- ‡ You have permitted them to drive in front of you.
- ‡ You smile at the guy collecting shopping carts.
- ‡ You gave him permission to smile back or to engage in a brief hello.
- ‡ You see the man from the Salvation Army ringing his bell.
- ‡ You avert your eyes—you held back permission because you didn't want to feel uncomfortable as you walked past without donating change.
- ‡ You pass other shoppers and acknowledge some with a nod.
- ‡ Yup, you gave them permission to return your gesture.
- ‡ An older man in a wheelchair, with his cart filled with frozen dinners, needs something from the top shelf. You have a choice to make. Do you break the silence and offer to help him select something outside of his reach?

- ‡ If you ask, you will likely get a thank you and possibly a story from his life. Are you going to give that permission away?
- ‡ What about the lady at the prescription counter? Are you going to ask her about the sling on her arm? It keeps her from quickly ringing up your medication.
- ‡ Is bringing kindness to her day going to provide uncomfortable permission for you?

I marked ‡ the moments you gave permission away so you could see just how quickly that permission slips through your fingers and how many times a day you give it away. It's a lot! And if you're introverted or a kind, peace-making, caregiver-type person, you might just be exhausting yourself with how often you grant permission to others.

How did your string hold up?

Did you have moments of hesitation?

Scenario #2

Permission with strangers is something we can easily give or withhold. It doesn't cost us much either way. Do you share the same permission with your child in the cereal aisle? Let's test the idea. Don't forget to unwind the string if the scenario presents a place you would choose to say yes, placing the next move in someone else's hands.

- ‡ Are you going to allow them to make an unhealthy cereal choice?
- ‡ Will they be allowed to choose something nobody else in your home will eat?
- ‡ Are you okay spending $7 for a box of cereal when the $3 generic box sits next to it?
- ‡ Can they select what they want just because there is a toy inside?
- ‡ If the child cries until they get what they want, will you give in?

How was your string experience different between the two scenarios? Are you a pushover with some people in your life? Do you find "no" a hard word to say?

Permission is a two-way street. As parents, friends, spouses, coworkers, and caregivers, we give and take permission without a second thought. The key to being relationally intelligent is understanding what to do when others give you (or don't give you) permission. You increase your emotional capacity when you learn from the best.

If someone withholds permission to engage, you must know how to avoid injury and diffuse the situation. That's a whole different type of skill. Then there are those tricky people that send mixed messages. You know the ones who bait you—leaving you trapped without options. Unsafe people lie in wait for you to respond incorrectly so they can manipulate your vulnerability with an inappropriate response. These toxic, untrustworthy people are in a cycle of inflicting pain. A wise person can discern some of the traps or pitfalls in these dangerous moments, but nobody is immune from getting hurt by risky people.

Here is where you might get stuck—permission giving can and might fail. That may seem obvious in some relationships and seem less potential with others. Your two-year-old can point out the flaws in your permission skills like a pro. Your mother may cross those barriers by way of a guilt trip, and your boss might journey across the line by asking for more than you can juggle.

The red-flag people in your life are those whose names are synonymous with the pain they inflict on you emotionally. You know exactly who they are. They reel you in like a fish on a hook, and when you take the bait, there should be warning bells clanging loudly. Each time they catch you on their hook, they have successfully surpassed your personal-permission boundaries. You might not have even recognized their crafty engagement as it slipped right past your best intentions. This decision is what we call a permission slip.

Pull yourself off their hook, humbled, ashamed, broken, or devastated, and you will have a moment in which you have to respond. You might find yourself in a situation where your quick wit causes a combination of words exiting your mouth with more force than respectability. Your actions might produce regretful memories, and your poorly intended responses might catch you in their sticky web. Engaging with risky people is not worth your time. They have figured out how to control the situation whether you engage or not. And even if you don't take part in their manipulation schemes, you have to keep your cool if you want to walk away intact.

If you've been tricked, if you've avoided the situation, you have an opportunity to express your character. Be very careful! Even if they have been awful toward you, you do not have permission to be a horrible person in return. Do not return anger with anger; manipulation with manipulation; or unkind words with unkind words.

Let me say that again. I don't want you to miss this—you don't have permission to be a jerk to anybody.

The moment you alter tactics, your sense of self-control can crumble. When you are angry, losing your control takes energy, it takes focus, and it takes your eye off what you should be focused on. When we get angry at someone, there is a moment afterward that feels like you've revealed your inner self in a vulnerable way. You might experience shame or guilt if you chose to explode. For days, weeks, or even years afterward, you might experience residual resentment, and those experiences only make you feel worse about yourself. Even if they are somewhat justified, angry outbursts never provide the result you wish you could achieve.

Someone who maliciously attacked you or stripped your dignity away is no more worthy of your permission giving than those we've already talked about. You have the power of choice here and now. How much control are you willing to give away? To the person who hurt you, destroyed your reputation, bullied your child, cut you off in traffic, committed a crime against you—don't give them your anger, your engagement, your permission—they're not worth it!

When you give the wrong person permission to wound your heart, you're opening up the possibility that person will wound you again. If you fail to keep them from returning, you are essentially giving them permission to suck your dignity right out the door. It doesn't mean you like it, you want it, or you deserve it, but it does mean you have an unresolved permission problem.

In a heated argument, nobody is actually going to win, and neither person gets their way. The result is a practice in successfully wounding one another until one person gives in or walks away. Sometimes nobody is willing or able to walk away. An escalation that requires getting the police involved is a terrible way to discover the places your permission-giving skill has failed.

That scenario may be a bit extreme, but tension builds, a crisis happens, and intervention is required at the rate of 20,000 calls to 9-1-1 each day in America.[1] Not every situation ends violently, but humans are great at inflicting pain instead of working out their differences. In fact, the idea of responding without inflicting pain is quite unnatural. It's a process that is learned through practice.

---

[1] National Coalition Against Domestic Violence (2020). Domestic violence. Retrieved from https://assets.speakcdn.com/assets/2497/domestic_violence-2020080709350855.pdf?1596811079991.

From a very young age responding to others appropriately is something you've struggled with. Your childhood had countless opportunities to practice proper responses. Toddlers hit back when a friend strikes them. Kindergarteners stick their tongue out in disgust. Teenagers argue out of rebellion. This same behavior is no longer acceptable in adulthood. So why is fighting back with words something we consider as an appropriate response? It's not. Being right does not heal the situation.

Words may be your worst enemy. Before you gain control of your thoughts, they are flying out of your mouth. If you're a seasoned screamer, a common yeller, or an occasional exploder, you have had one of those moments you wish you could recapture and start over. Your words matter. The good ones, the bad ones, the underhanded ones, and the harsh ones too. You know that, but somehow you still wrestle with this one behavior you must gain control of. If you hope to heal from your wounds, you need to learn to be a person who helps others heal and one who reduces the wounds dished out.

Is there a way to fix a broken relationship without further wounds? There are places in our society where this ideal is lived out. Doctors hold one another accountable to the Hippocratic oath, pledging not to harm and act justly while caring for patients. Keeping them from hurting a patient or withholding care even to criminals. You may have heard teachings like, "love your enemies," or "do unto others as you would have them do unto you." This very philosophy is where the answer you are looking for lies, right smack in the middle of it. Simply stated, you need to be the bigger person.

Two principles govern your reactions to other people. How well you manage the permission you give others, and how intentionally you respond to those with whom you engage. But those two principles are among the most complicated actions known to humanity.

If you take nothing else out of the gift I've presented, take this: The moment you choose to control your response is the moment where you will experience freedom from any situation in which you engage. But beware! Trying to control the outcome, control people, control fear, or control chaos, you will see just how little power you have in the world. This is not an exercise or means of manipulation but instead acknowledges your ability to respond appropriately—*that* is what you *can* control.

God, grant me the serenity
to accept the things I cannot change,
the courage to change the things I can,
and the wisdom to know the difference.
Living one day at a time,
enjoying one moment at a time;
accepting hardship as a pathway to peace;
taking, as Jesus did,
this sinful world as it is,
not as I would have it;
trusting that You will make all things right
if I surrender to Your will;
so that I may be reasonably happy in this life
and supremely happy with You forever in the next.
Amen.
—Reinhold Niebuhr

Have you ever read the Serenity Prayer? It's a standard in every 12-step program. "God grant me the serenity to accept the things I cannot change, the courage to change the things I can, and the wisdom to know the difference…"

Keep that string handy. Any time you question your control of a situation, test it. Are you giving away the wrong permission? Do you want to control? Do you know the difference?

Journaling Opportunity

- Write out the Serenity Prayer. Pause and consider how it connects to your life.
- What are the things you need to accept?
- What are the things you cannot change?
- What do you need to do each day to choose to let go?
- What is keeping you from experiencing a lifestyle of freedom?

5

pesky pebbles and great big boulders

"Nothing in the Christian life is more important than forgiveness—our forgiveness of others and God's forgiveness of us."
—John F. MacArthur

RETURN WITH ME to the imaginary gift box with the red bow on top. Inside there is a rock, and it's actually a tiny pebble. I'd love for you to go a step beyond our previous hypothetical items and actually pick up a small rock outside and place it in your pocket, on your desk, or your dashboard as a reminder of this next conversation.

While telling me her life story, a staff member paused to tell me about her deepest regrets. Her mother had tragically passed away, but Shelly felt relieved. Although she felt shame and guilt for her feelings, she couldn't move on. Her hatred for her mom had destroyed their relationship and left her with obsessive thoughts about the past. As an outsider looking in, you can quickly question what dysfunctional experiences revolved around the permission she gave her mom. Even in the grave, Shelly's mom was inflicting pain. Shelly had not stopped permitting her mother to have control. She was letting things she couldn't change have free reign to taint her daily life.

When my mom was diagnosed with a terminal illness, Shelly looked me in the eye and challenged me to respond differently. If she could go back, she would have taken the high road, would have been the bigger person, spent quality time, and lovingly invested in those tough conversations that had been scooted under the rug. Though it was too late for her to go back and address her source of pain, she wanted to keep me from doing the same.

Before you dismiss Shelly's story, there is another detail I'd like you to observe. Shelly had done a great thing by intervening in my life, and she could have stopped there. She could have given up because her mom was gone, allowing regret to burrow in and make her bitter; or she could choose to figure out a way to forgive herself for missed opportunities. A strategic letter to her mother allowed her to say the things she missed but provided a way for her to share those regrets therapeutically. Shelly no longer gives her mom permission to rob the future with memories from the past.

One of the best choices of my life was getting on the next plane and spending a few days with my parents. Before that conversation, I had exactly zero interest in visiting with them. Presence is something we withhold from others when we are wounded. Giving your presence to someone is one of the most forward ways of starting the forgiveness conversation. If you will choose to be present, you can model what that looks like for those who were not present for you.

Sometimes we can revisit the place where our wounds began. We can address them with the people who delivered them. But even if you can't, there are ways to move forward, and you may need to vary your approach. I would encourage you to identify the moment each pain on your lifelong scorecard began. That might help you consider if you have the ability to go back and address it.

I was fortunate enough to have those face-to-face conversations. Since then I have tried to live a regret-free life. It doesn't always work—and when I mess it up, neglect to make the right decision, or cause pain to another person, I make a point of assessing the situation and considering where things are not working.

An interesting observation is that communication is often the center of my failed decision-making, and I am then obligated to step up and fix the problem. It has become my goal to work it out. It might not be today or this week, but in time, I have learned that working out the emotional baggage I carry is worth the effort again and again. I've also noticed that I have the urge to flee when I'm unwilling to face difficult circumstances. Fight or flight is a common term used for how we address conflict. Are you more inclined to fight for yourself, or to run from the reality that pain is around the corner?

Sometimes we fall into traps of pain because we believe that forgiveness means forgetting. Forgetting what you've been through is not the same as forgiving the person who wronged you. For those of us who struggle with conflict resolution, this is more than just walking in the opposite direction from a problem. This is not simply forgetting about an incident where the pain was inflicted; this is choosing to find a place where the resolution sits comfortably inside daily living.

You may be saying, "I couldn't forgive ________, it's too ________." That act is not for the weak, but I assure you forgiveness really is possible. And you may resist the idea that permission has been given to someone who abusively violated you. In no way am I blaming you for being in the wrong place at the wrong time or for taking on something unthinkable. But your response is what you have control over, which means your ability to forgive is inside of your control.

When an action is so significant that it could ruin your life, forgiveness may be the last thing you would ever consider. I've been on the receiving end, and I'm familiar with that battle. I remember hearing someone say, "The truth will set you free," and the truth is, the bigger the act, the more captive it can take your life as if it has sent a ransom letter to your heart which never got paid. Burying this deeply and throwing away the key is the type of permission that will eat you from the inside out. If the act of aggression that caused the pain doesn't destroy you, self-inflicted disdain for others will give it a try.

Harbored inside of you are varying levels of hatred waiting for the perfect moment to be granted an escape making a center-stage appearance. Those are the moments you see in the rearview mirror and wish you could magically erase. Good character is never present in such a messy scene. Even if it is justified, malice will rob you of joy, peace, generosity, love, sleep, physical pleasure, tangible experiences, laughter, and connectedness in other relationships.

The bubbling up of hurt feelings and unexplainable emotions are like pebbles in your shoes. A tiny pebble on a long hike can derail even the most seasoned hiker. Take the pebble out, and immediately the journey gets more enjoyable. Become a shoe-stone collector, and your trip is wrecked before it even begins.

Flip back to the Regret Influence Chart you created in chapter 2. I want you to envision each item on that list as a single pebble. The higher your score, the bigger the rock. Consider each as an isolated bother. It can slow you down, cause more pain, influence the growth of calluses created to protect you from more pain, and if time is allowed to hold them over, they will surely produce significant complications. You must attend to these stones! That means it's time to take off your shoes and dump out the contents. The journey ahead is too vital for you to keep giving those pebbles permission to wound you further.

Walk around with shoes overflowing with rock, sand, or gravel, and you will have forgotten how to walk (live) altogether. Nursing blistered feet is a reaction to a problem that could have been avoided much earlier. Giving in and allowing fear, pain, anxiety, depression, burnout, exhaustion, illness, and neglect to run life is the very definition of dysfunction, so don't settle.

Have you ever bumped into someone who has learned to love the actual crisis they live within? Before long, you realize they are addicted to the struggle. Avid wilderness adventurers know the dangers of traveling alone. Having a partner in the journey may be what they need to successfully discover the problem with their rock-to-shoe ratio. This is also a reminder that you need to listen when friends lovingly remind you of your own shortcomings. You may have already identified someone else who needs to read this right now.

While we're talking about investing in others, remember that not everyone is ready to hear what you have to offer. You're learning new skills, but your spouse and kids might not understand. In my line of work I frequently help parents who rearrange their children's lives before assessing their own. The urge to help someone through a life overhaul is a strong one. But before you overreact, take off your shoes and drop out a few of your rocks as you read through the truths below.

1. Hard times make us better people.
2. Work hard; it pays off.
3. (Almost always) We need to be the ones to solve the problem, so we appreciate the work it took to get it right.
4. Bailing kids (or other family members) out of consequences cheats them out of life experience, resiliency, and problem-solving skills.
5. Preparation for successful adulthood is the purpose of childhood.
6. Hard things don't come easily, and you'll never feel like doing them, so just start. Get going, move forward, do it—the rewards will come in unexpected places. Live expectantly.
7. Adults don't get to have snow days from life. Life doesn't stop when there are storms. Learn to be tough and push through. Don't look for the easy way out.
8. Choose to believe the best in others and relieve yourself from being easily offended. Easily offended people are resentful of hard things and hard times. You've already learned that resentment is possibly the most destructive entity in your life—right up there with regret.

9. Setting priorities helps us filter investment risk, but it doesn't eliminate regret. Maturity allows us to invest wisely, promote living a life of productivity, and contribute to the community around us.
10. The same people that limit you are hoping you will give them limited permission.
11. If you have healthy relationships, you will see them pay off in every area of your life.
12. The key to happy living, free of weights and expectations, is finding contentment in what you can't control.

My final thought: *You* are equipped, and *you* are capable.

Journaling Opportunity

It's time to assess these twelve rules of healthy adulting. (I'm sure there are more.)

- How are you doing with the items on this list?
- Choose one that you struggle with the most. Please write a few thoughts about it.

- Choose the one you think you've mastered. Are you setting that example for the people around you? For your kids? Your coworkers? For those you influence?
- What control seeking do you need to give up?

Understanding pain, regret, forgiveness, and resentment is not the key to obtaining freedom, but there are benefits to dissecting their structure. Vast amounts of time could be spent trying to untangle senseless "why" questions when you could be reframing them by asking, "What's next?" or "What matters most?" Change the questions you are asking if you are looking for freedom and you'll experience a new perspective, equipping you to live without regret. It will be worth it!

6

the past

"What if the thing that produces your pain is the very thing that God will use to release His power?"
—Steven Furtick

LIFE'S LITTLE MOMENTS present themselves like a stack of photographs tied to sensory recordings in the mind. The right brain and left brain work together to file the entire collection with facts and logical sensations. Try to connect these dots and you'll discover that your creative side has smudged a few lines, changed the connections, or even erased undesirable elements. When the files are retrieved as a complete package, they make sense.

When you dig back through the file cabinet of your mind, you may be surprised by the different versions of the story you remember. Talk to others who were there and they may have recorded different or additional details, facts, or sensations. This explains why the courtroom process is so important. Ask lots of witnesses and the complete picture can be painted.

Open your memory files and you'll notice more than just colorful pictures inside. Recognizing detailed fragments of sight, smell, touch, sound, and feelings associated with the facts is what makes memory useful. Closing your eyes and breathing deeply may help you pinpoint the influence of a single historical event. Hollywood has featured this experience in countless scenes because everyone wants the superpower of time travel.

If only you could sort past the cinnamon smell of a candle, the warmth of the oven, the bitter cold of a park bench, the noise of the crowd, arriving at the exact detail you'd like to change. Then what? I've yet to meet a single person who has obsessed over the past enough to wake up one day harnessing the power to alter the details.

The filing system of the brain is mysterious. Your magnificently designed brain didn't come with a "fix the past" mode, yet more often than you might notice, your longings are for just such a thing. Much like in the past, you don't have that much control of what your brain stores or what it recalls.

There is a difference between stored thought and recalled thinking. Think of your messy desk. Where did you put that paper? Recall is the ability to find it and storage is the ability to keep it. Digging through the past is necessary to produce a memory. Sometimes the details are stuffed in the wrong drawer or covered in coffee stains.

Search through your memory bank and things may not add up. Your recall mode may present facts as fragmented details which have shaped your past or present self. At times your memory can be a frame-by-frame recall of the situation. The difference is hard to distinguish. Good memories are not the only ones recorded. The search may conjure up some facts you've hidden quite well. Scientists are studying this process to understand it more.

Notice the connections between your senses and your memories. A sound might reintroduce a feeling of rage or fear. Like a photograph, the image contains details connected to emotions. When you record emotions, there is no photograph-style filing tool available to use. Memories are feelings expressed as experiences, and they are not always explainable. They can enhance or distort your recollection of the past, and that's not always a good thing.

Understanding the past is something we wish for almost as much as changing it. My journey into the past is a mixture of curiosity, observation, exploration, and pain—lots of pain. My earliest memory is quite vivid: red lights on top of trucks, men with hoses, billowing clouds, and so many people working together. A dump truck stood ready with sand to extinguish the chemically induced flames. Four tiny eyes peered through the glass in awe of the activity in the garage. I've often wished the rest of my childhood fed my curiosity at that level.

There were lots of moments of wonder in our home. We learned to feed our curiosity with never-ending questions. Taking things apart and reengineering their usefulness was a game. And then there were moments where confusion, chaos, and incomprehensible photographs were stored.

I've never been much of a photographer, but even I know that overexposed film, fingers in front of lenses, and pocket shots are worthless. Much of my childhood could be explained with similar images. Don't get me wrong, growing up at our house wasn't all bad—but the secrets we kept were pretty awful.

The most challenging parts of my early years started with touching, then undressing, and before long sexual abuse, which stole the rest of my innocent years. With more than one aggressor in my home, I can't really remember a time I felt safe, but there were some good memories nonetheless. As a result of confusing roles and manipulated aggression, I grew up with a relatively twisted idea of relationships. I learned to interpret other people's actions completely wrong, and I struggled with insecurity, significance, and the need to negotiate my validity. My mother and I never really connected, and my father had a lot of anger and rage incidents. This album of distorted images plagues my desire to fix the past.

Right or wrong, my own parenting decisions have been much gentler, more question-centered, and much more like life coaching than discipline. We asked our kids to reframe their decisions in the rearview mirror. What could they have done differently? What choices should they have made? This perspective helped them look backward at mistakes and gain skills to apply forward in decision-making. We certainly aren't perfect parents, and we've had our share of bad decision-making, but comparing my childhood with my parenting is not even remotely similar.

I can attribute much of that success to my husband, who has taken this journey like a champ. He knew my life was a mess when we met, but he is often surprised when I reveal a detailed piece from the mountain of pain. The best thing he has taught me is how to use memories to shape the future. I may not be able to change what has happened, but I sure can find use in those experiences going forward. Bad examples are still examples, and every life lesson has an opportunity for growth.

Life has given me so many opportunities to practice the skills of self-patience and self-forgiveness that I need to function on an optimal level. I've learned to model grace and mercy, and I've discovered the importance of functioning inside the practical end of forgiveness on a daily basis.

I'd love to challenge you to find people who can be your example setters, your accountability, your supporters. Whether they are your group or your person, they will make you a better version of yourself.

Let's talk quickly about what their role is not. It's not about gossip; it's not about a place to sit around and retell your story over and over and stew upon unresolved conflict. This crew is your grow-out-of-dysfunction support group—even if they don't know it. That's what friends are for. Don't overindulge or become too clingy, and don't overwhelm them. They don't have the "fix it" button either, but they can support you going forward.

When you don't know the answer, where do you turn? Search engines have made a business out of your despair. They don't know what you don't know, but they can help you find out. That's exactly what your group can do. Their skill set is most valuable when they use words like *no, stop, quit,* and *I love you.* Their role includes holding you accountable when they see stubborn, impulsive, obsessive patterns.

Complicated moments cause the brain to stop processing the entire picture. In those moments survival kicks in and all bets are off. You have to let them speak to you honestly, lovingly, and directly when that happens. Their influence, partnered with your commitment to your growth, will see your tendencies change. A rebellious decision will change to cooperation and contribution. Depressed or discouraged thinking will turn to optimism and positivity. And permission giving will turn to well-thought-out relationship connections.

What is your role? First and foremost, get positive and stay hopeful. Invest in your success. Be open; share with honesty, integrity, and courage. Welcome others to energize and strengthen you. Listen, allowing them to speak wisdom into your world. Invite them to model function in places you tend toward dysfunction. Don't spoil or tarnish those relationships. They are priceless, and they are much harder to build than to keep.

Yesterday should not be wasted. It's full of fuel to make the future extraordinary. You can control the measuring stick you use to determine the success that lies ahead. Your decisions will define who you are, but just because you have a lousy track record or because someone else's decisions have ruined a portion of your life—it's not over! You are much more than any one of those decisions. And you are much more than the sum-total of all your decisions.

Journaling Opportunity

1. What lies have you accepted?
2. What abuse, misinformation, manipulation, or mistreatment have you endured that you've tucked away for another day?
3. What excuses have you made for the way you have held onto the pain?

4. Have you decided it's your fault, that speaking up won't make a difference, or that you're not worthy of better? What other lies have you expressed in your head?
5. When do you tend to run away and not face the truth?
6. Who is in your grow-out-of-dysfunction support group?
7. Is there anyone in your life dragging you down?
8. Who should be added or removed from your inner circle?
9. What photograph in your memory is your favorite? Tell somebody about it.

7

wounds

"Listen, God, I'm calling at the top of my lungs:
'Be good to me! Answer me!'
When my heart whispered, 'Seek God,'
my whole being replied,
'I'm seeking him!'
Don't hide from me now!
You've always been right there for me;
don't turn your back on me now.
Don't throw me out, don't abandon me"
(Psalm 27:9-10, MSG).

THE FLOOR WAS cold as I slipped my five-year-old foot out of bed and onto the squishy carpet below. Slinking through the hallway, I stood silently as my curious mind wanted to take it all in. The gifts under the tree were so enticing. I couldn't wait. The magic of Christmas would surely make today spectacular!

My next step would end the euphoric thinking for a time. Lying on the floor, I found my thoughts racing. My mind wondered two things. What had I slipped on, and why was this plastic brick lying on the floor? Like an alarm clock, the wailing of my cries woke the family and the magical moment disappeared from the room. If you look closely you can still make out the letters O-G-E-L on my right temple.

A wound is a description for anything from a paper cut to the most traumatic vision you can conjure. A few years ago I arrived at the bedside of my brother, who lay on a hospital bed connected to a ventilator. The destruction of his face via a self-inflicted gunshot wound had taken the place of his formerly strong jawline and well-pronounced cheekbone. Surgeons collected what they could, repaired what they were able, and methodically began creating what was missing. Metal plates, screws, and colorful wires were visible as his body slowly began the healing process. At first even the doctors thought his wounds might be too large to heal.

Your creativity is needed for just a moment as we imagine that box with the big red bow. It's time to sort through and find the bandage inside. Since you're the one imagining the bandage, you can create any image you'd like. It can be a huge piece of gauze—large enough to wrap a skyscraper, or it can be a tiny plastic strip made perfectly for the knee of a stumbling toddler.

Take a moment to assess the wounds you've collected in your lifetime. A pesky cut on the side of your finger quickly reminds you of its presence when it's dipped in dishwater or as you peel an orange. Small, large, or somewhere in between, the distracting voice of a wound can speak loudly. The treatment may be as simple as an ice pack or a bandage, and sometimes hope and prayer are all you've got. Some wounds declare their unwillingness to heal long after you've forgotten the source of injury.

My emotional wounds started earlier than I can remember. Their distress signals were the occasional cause for a therapy visit. The more persistent pain could be brushed off like an arthritic knee on a cold day. I had to arrive at the point of impasse before I would address it. One of the people I needed to forgive was no longer living, another was in prison, and the other had created so much fear I struggled to process the mixed messages sent by way of manipulation and rejection. Though a therapist could talk through my issues, I experienced a lack of resolution and a validated sense of abandonment.

Each person who has deeply wounded you must be addressed. The result will be monumental. You can stop being ignored, criticized, put down, abused, or taken advantage of. When that person is not accessible, you can't give them a chance to accept your forgiveness. It's in this setting you might want to consider a surrogate. In order to work through the pain, you may need to find someone who will act as the individual who wronged you so you can actively go through the process of giving forgiveness. Even the pain you have connected to someone unreachable can be dealt with.

When your perpetrator instills fear associated with their rage, their control may have removed your voice. Your courage can be exhibited when you move past the pounding in your chest that's synonymous with a lack of air in your lungs. Walking uphill against the flood of agonizing memories can be elaborately debilitating. Instinctively you must fight through tears, confusion, and shreds of mental images that remain as if they commemorate a historically significant event. Some people awaken from the worst dreams only to discover they are reality.

If you are presently assuming the proverbial fetal position, your relationship with fear is more than an acquaintance. Perpetuated anxiety can be the source of hidden wounds that keep popping open. Devastating results can manifest with emotional incisions that never seem to heal.

Identifying your pain may be easily done through a self-diagnostic approach. But don't simply label it and move on. The examination is not the end result. Think of your pain like a starting line in a race where the finish line is liberation.

Consider the latitude of this wound. It's yours, and it is unique in power, in the ability to paralyze, and in the flexibility you give it to remain functional. It's not like anything else we've talked about. Process your fears associated with its internal impact. Take it out, hold it in your hands. Think about where it came from.

Are you ready to get rid of it?

This exercise was created for you to return to any time you need it.

- Take a deep breath.
- Hold it in.
- Close your eyes for a moment.

- Process it. Take as long as you need.
- Take another breath and feel that pain, regret, overwhelmingness, anxiety, depression—whatever that mixture of feeling is—it's sabotaging you. And it's not going to quit.
- Is this wound too big to heal from?
- Let your lungs feel the cleansing energy of your breath.
- Savor it.
- Hang on and let your mind contemplate what it would be like if that pain went away.
- Would it be okay?
- Would you regret it being removed from your life?
- How else could you be using all the energy it sucks from you?
- Have you tucked it so far down that it only pops up on occasion?
- What makes you think of it?
- Can you imagine taking it in your hands, holding it like a tangible object, and placing it in a box?
- What if you could mail that box to an undisclosed location where it would be destroyed?

You can! And that's what this book is about.

There's no rule dictating how big or little a past memory is, and likewise, there's no one way to deal with all of them. Figuratively they can each have their own box in which to be sent away.

I can confidently say you will be a different person without those wounds. Are you ready to give all of them up, and not just the ones that are small enough to put a bandage on?

I'd like to encourage you here—there are many stepping-stones in your lifelong journey, including people you trust, counselors, doctors, therapists, pastors, and even this book. Each one can also have an important role in your healing. Don't go it alone. Relationships may be the source of pain, but they are also the source of healing. Find a support system. If you have to, build one and rely upon it. If you have faith—lean into it.

I am an introvert, and the thought of telling my story to another human is unsettling. My journey includes a therapist, a girlfriend group that is second to none, a supportive family, and a faith that has seen mountains move. Those relationships need to be cultivated, nurtured, and grown. Healthy support systems don't just pop up overnight.

I'm convinced not everyone will have that type of village supporting them. But I do know a great therapist is a good starting point. One thing I've learned from Jeremy (my therapist) is that my significance matters, and the work I do on the train ride through my healing process will influence others. For me, that is significant. I care about others, and I find the people I care most about are benefiting from my emotional and mental health. Building your support system is a lot to think about. Take a few minutes away and consider who those people are. How can you build that team? What type of people do you need to add to your friend group?

Your wounds have a way of taking over life—every single breath. The people you surround yourself with have the ability to push you forward or pull you back down. The ones worth investing in will hold you accountable, they will push you when you don't think you can keep going, and they will hold you up when you need it most. Don't forget; they need your presence too. Be sure to be a contributor to every relationship you're in.

Relational cuts, scrapes, and bruises are part of being human. How you share your wound experience allows you to begin living with authenticity. The cycles of pain you have allowed to build (voluntarily or involuntarily) are stopping you from the transparency needed to grow. If you want to learn to trust, learn to love, and learn to care for others more than you already do, address the life-threatening wounds in your life. Pack them up and get ready for the next step in the process.

Journaling Opportunity

- Envision your heartbreaks, hurts, and your disappointments.
- You can even draw them if you'd like.
- If they were wounds, what would they look like?
- What type of surgery, bandage, or splint would be needed to hold them together while they heal?
- Have you tried to perform your own plastic surgery to hide the wounds?
- Do you notice the same wound hanging on for a long time?
- Have you repeated the same wound care over and over? Why?

8

vicious cycles

"God rescued us from dead-end alleys and dark dungeons. He's set us up in the kingdom of the Son he loves so much, the Son who got us out of the pit we were in, got rid of the sins we were doomed to keep repeating"
(Colossians 1:14, MSG).

THIS CHAPTER FEATURES a new item in the gift box of forgiveness symbols. It's a sweet, soft little hamster. (Aren't you glad these are virtual treasures?)

I think we've known each other long enough to smile and laugh a little. When my children were in elementary school, they asked for a hamster. And of course, being the caring mom, I even gave permission for two rodents to join our already large family. The nice lady at the pet store assured us that both were boys. Two short weeks later, the kids were so excited when they woke up to six tiny hairless babies nestled in a single ball. Evidently neither Fred nor Spot were boys. We had purchased not one but two pregnant hamsters, and as you guessed it, just one day later Spot produced another half-dozen family members.

Mass production capabilities of rodents became a harsh reality. Twenty-one days had passed and the stench of the rodent household had pushed me over the edge. Babies or not, I was determined to erase every slice of wood shaving that harbored odor. The attention span of a homeschooled rodent watcher is pretty short when aggression breaks out in full display for the world. That, followed by the announcement that Spot was building a new nest, troubled me. Even the cutest hamster has limits when it comes to interrupting schoolwork. I covered the cage with a towel so the kids could focus.

The surprise on my face was anything but positive that afternoon. Pulling back the cover, the kids exposed not just Spot and Fred with their month-old litters, but also a new set of children, which had magically appeared. By 2:00 p.m. we had fifty-six sweet, soft, cuddly hamsters. For the record, that is not an exaggeration. We couldn't give hamsters away fast enough. The hamster ball, a few hamster wheels, tunnels, and cages filled our garage. It was like a giant circus, and though it was cute for a while, it was far from under control.

Every month every female could produce a litter, and some mommies delivered in less than three weeks. We were on the brink of a nuclear hamster explosion. We were stuck in a hamster breeding zone fit for a scene in a horror movie, and there was absolutely no way to get ahead of the breeding curve. Rodents had overtaken our garage, and it took less than three months to be so far out of control that we had to seek professional help.

Now that you've laughed at my expense and forbidden your children from ever purchasing a rodent at a pet shop, I want you to think about your disastrous problems and the speed at which they replicate. Our rodent problem went from zero to sixty so fast that steering wasn't an option. Ironically, the cycle we had gotten into was like the proverbial hamster wheel, and getting off was the thing of nightmares. Can you relate?

Thankfully humans don't have babies at the same rate rodents do! In fact, your life is much different in every way. Rodents don't have jobs, drive cars, go to college, or have birthday parties. They don't learn algebra, read books, or travel to foreign countries. The simplicity of their lives helps us to be grateful for the possibilities we have. In that simplistic arena, there are no relationship troubles, trauma specialists, or forgiveness tools either. You may dream of such basic requirements, but that's not possible. You are human, and that means life is demanding, and you don't just have one hamster wheel at any given time. You've got a variety of shapes, sizes, and speeds on which you can run. Most days the choice is yours, and if you locate the right set of wheels in the proper sequence, you'll come out standing upright.

Your life is anything but simple. Your very existence isn't even ordinary. You are not here by accident. Let's start there. Just you being on earth is evidence that you matter. Don't for a moment discount that.

If you're alive, you have successfully made it into the pool of over 7,200,000,000 earth dwellers on planet Earth. And if you are that lucky, you see the potential for countless relationships. Friendship with another living, breathing human being is beautiful. Your support for one another breeds strength; the hamsters taught us that. But unlike hamsters, you have the power to choose who you will spend time with and which ones will be given the privilege to have your influence. When selecting your significant friend(s), look for the strongest and be wary of the most powerful.

Remember our conversation on permission giving? With friends, you must carefully control the influence exchange rate. There is wisdom in a careful selection of your inner circle so that influence is easier to manage. Healthy friendships exhibit interactions that make you a better person. The hamster cage also serves as a reminder of the potential for the shock you might experience if a dysfunctional relationship has grown out of control.

What dysfunction? If you're always giving and never receiving, or if you are experiencing the same dysfunction you want to avoid, you may be repeating the cycle of bad relationship selection. One choice is to go back to the pool of 7,200,000,000+ and start over. Or change your approach with the current selection.

If you want to commit to making the current relationships worthwhile, some things have to change. Communication is a good place to start. You need people that support you mutually—don't forget that piece. You need those with the ability to stop your spinning habits, and you need those who will love you unconditionally through the process.

You don't need significance depleters, and you don't need people unwilling to give and accept forgiveness in appropriate spaces. So be sure you consider wisely before committing to any relationship. Optimism plays a complementary role as well. Believe the best in people, give them the benefit of the doubt, and allow yourselves to grow in maturity together.

The worst part of a relationship gone wrong is the leftover messages you keep in your collection of dysfunction. They are quietly spilling into your unconscious thoughts, and at the perfect time, they jump out and say things like: "You weren't good enough for ____, so you're not good enough for anyone." or "If you had only ______, you would still be in a relationship with _____."

These lies ooze with insignificance. Misused, they bring on overwhelming feelings of insecurity. Words and the actions of others destroy positivity if used inappropriately. The mind uses sleight of hand to take a great person and convince them of their insignificance. Those messages can call to you like the hamster wheel waiting to be spun. Get on the wheel and you are taking a gamble with the outcome.

Let's examine the wheel of thoughts you are working with:

- Wound (The moment where someone else hurts you deeply)
- Pain (The result of the wound. The pain sits in your heart, mind, and emotions.)

- Negative thought processes that internalize by damaging your self-image
- Feeding the wound with self-pity or poor coping mechanisms
- Expressing thoughts like *I'll never* _______ (inner words you say that stick in your mind)
- Resentment
- Nurtured resentment (more self-pity and poor coping)
- Weaponized resentment (turning your pain/anger/resentment onto others)
- Returning the favor of the wound by inflicting unkind words, emotions, manipulation, or gestures.

These can happen in a few moments or can take weeks to unfold. Either way, your response is what you are responsible for.

Any curious person finds themself mesmerized by the dedication of a hamster to operate the spinning machine that simply wastes energy and leads to nowhere. The higher the velocity of the spin, the more traumatic the moment of exit can be. The longer we run, the more we realize we're going nowhere. The more we ponder, obsess, or try to renegotiate the "should have," "would have," or "could have" moments, the more the vicious cycle continues. Each time you reengage with a person who feeds the lies increases the velocity of the wheel or wastes your time. You are perpetuating the vicious cycle. Unlike the hamster, you know better, and you can get off and stay off.

The right people can change the should/would/could messages you're spinning and replace them with the questions you should be asking instead.

- What's healthy?
- What's next?
- What matters most?

You know them by now, and you just need to enforce them with the right frame of mind. One single "I wish I could go back and change…." idea can weigh you down and start the wheel rolling all over again.

When you're sure you are ready to be off for good, don't call that friend that will join you on the wheel and run with you. And most definitely don't call that friend who likes to stop their own wheel only to experience their body being flung round and round until it stops. I know I've taken the metaphor too far, but I couldn't resist. We've all got that crazy friend, and this is not where they come into the healthy picture.

The straightest line from point A (where you are) to point B (where you want to be) is dismantling the various parts of your spinning thought patterns. Taking back permission could save your life. Embrace facts, have faith, believe there is more to living, and choose to feel better. Cycling at full throttle may be emotionally raw with personal significance at risk. Reduce internalizing of misguided messages that sound like: *I hate myself, I'm not worthy, I deserved it, I'm weak, I should have known better.* Living into those lies can reverse the process all too quickly.

Here is a better way to handle the situation:

- Consider what has gotten you stuck.
- What is so overwhelming or makes you think about quitting?
- Think of something that symbolizes your pain or a significant part of the vicious cycle.
- Picture it vividly. (Make it a hamster if you'd like).
- Write a letter to the pain, to the offender, or yourself. Speak freely. Cry. Share your anger. DO NOT

DELIVER THAT MESSAGE if you wrote it to someone else!

- Decide what action you should take.
- Spend some time grieving the past. Permit yourself to cry some more.
- You might like to destroy the symbolic item you created.
- Decide that you won't give that item or memory the permission to continue feeding the messages, the photographs, or the wounds you remember.
- Wind up that string and take back the permission you should never have given away.

The symbol I chose was a mirror. I didn't like the person I could see in the glass. Adopting negative words and abusing them was my vicious cycle. After I had been sexually assaulted, "I deserved it," "I am worthless," and many more phrases rooted deeply in my heart. I wrote three separate letters that I burned. I cried—a lot—and broke the mirror. I hated cleaning up the glass, but I found healing in the gesture.

Your response to each step is your choice. The significance you give away is yours to own. Notice I didn't say control. I said own. Remember the Serenity Prayer. There are things I can't change or control.

Giving up control, submitting to the idea that I couldn't fix things, and releasing harbored resentment brought me to the place where I was ready to forgive. I just never expected the process to be so much about me.

I was a tarnished individual, and I needed a personal voice so I could speak the forgiveness that needed to be heard. A friend heard my heart and coached my actions. There was something therapeutic about sharing the words I couldn't say directly to my perpetrator. The crazy thing is, I see myself completely different now. It's amazing what a little permission to grieve and let go can do.

Another surprising result was inside the good relationships in my life. No longer talking about negativity has opened the door for deeper conversation. I have better friends because I have the energy to be a better friend. I'm a better mom, wife, and employee as well. All of that negative energy was reduced, and Julie 2.0 replaced the hamster wheel-racing woman that once thrived inside chaotic environments. There are still people who hurt me, but I find myself giving less permission for that pain to dig so deeply. I've learned to say "stop" when someone is making me uncomfortable, and I've formed habits that directly speak to people when they are attempting to create pain in my life.

Here's a new and improved Pain-Reduction Cycle.

↓ Wound initiated
↓ Permission to destroy taken back (string wound up tightly)
↓ The decision to see my significance or give it away is objectively held up
↓ A solid decision to not allow it to take root in my life
↓ The decision to disable inner words that enter the scene
↓ Empowerment
↓ Intentional optimism instead of resentment
↓ Deweaponized response
↓ Active decision to forgive and let go

In rewriting your process, you will see how powerful it is to remove the control others once lorded over you. In a sense, you have used the alarm system you created. It cautioned you to take notice, and it motivated you to change the outcome. You have effectively taken permission away from the wrong set of hands.

I'm happy to tell you that we did get our rodent farm under control, and we stopped letting the craziness grow out of control. The significance of that memory keeps me from making the same bad choice again. We started this chapter by talking about two types of significance. The first is the significance of decision-making, and the second is the significance of fixing the problem. You can get off that hamster wheel in your life, and you can do it successfully. It may be complicated, and you may have a few dozen problematic offspring to unload, but you have the tools!

There's more good news—the end of your story has not been reached. Rewrite your destiny, fill it with correct messages, and ensure relationships bring the right type of significance. Choose to be physically and emotionally present and contribute to a better you.

Journaling Opportunity

- Take five minutes to consider what you want the end of your story to be. Not the end of your life, but the end of this single dart of pain that digs deeper than any other. Do you see a way to take it out?

- Can you visualize yourself changing the vicious cycle into a Pain Reduction Cycle, even if it is just with one person in your life?
- Finally, write the name of the person you want to ask, "When can I count on you?"

9

significance

"At that point, Peter got up the nerve to ask, 'Master, how many times do I forgive a brother or sister who hurts me?' "
(Matthew 18:21, MSG).

CAN YOU CONFIDENTLY answer the question, "Who are you?" Try this trick. Read it three times and each time emphasize a different word. *Who* are you? Who *are* you? Who are *you?* Did that provide changing perspectives?

Knowing who you are, who you want to be, and who others think you are is a difficult balancing act. Tip the scale in any direction and it's off-balance.

The way you answer the question says a lot. The day I learned about the depth of the messages I was speaking internally I realized it was up to me to reconsider the way I balanced my self-image. Standing in the bathroom,

I gazed into the mirror, and not only did I not like the person I saw, but I also didn't even recognize the reflection in front of me.

When you look in the mirror, who is it that you see? What are your honest thoughts about the view?

Inside this gift box I have placed a virtual mirror. Like the other items—it's for you. Do you remember the story of the stepmother that looked in the mirror and asked who was the fairest in the land? I can't help but wonder if she asked that question because she didn't believe the mirror when it announced her beauty. Was it possible that she didn't like the image of herself?

Eyes are said to be the window of the soul. As a teenager, did you ever gaze into your own eyes? What about now? Do they express a message for the world? Look past the outer appearance of your own image right now. Do your other features reflect what's going on inside your heart? Inside your head? Inside the words you speak or the actions you portray? Is that really you? Does it reveal happiness, sadness, confusion, or chaotic thoughts? What would you prefer for it to reveal?

Every single day you interact with people, and each one of them gets a little different view. Your friends see one side of you that is not likely the same as the one you reveal to your boss, your pastor, or your mother. Your kids see a more realistic side, and your spouse sees you more in-depth than any of the others. Are you controlling what they see? Is that person authentically you? Or are you working so hard to cover up the real person that you don't even see who you have become?

Walk through the self-care aisles at the store and you'll discover a multibillion-dollar industry that increases the image you portray. I'm always amazed at the cost when I fill my shopping cart with deodorant, body wash, makeup, cologne, jewelry, clothing, shoes, eyewear, and other beautifying products. I have friends who invest in Botox and tummy tucks, weight loss shakes or shots, and those who go to the gym religiously. Who are we trying to impress?

Have you ever considered exactly what is at the root of what you're covering up? What is it that is so important for you to alter? What perceptions of yourself are you forcing others to have? And if you could stop covering up the negative parts of yourself, would you?

I'll never forget the day my coworker came to the office with curly hair and no makeup. I didn't recognize her until she spoke to me. Her two-hour morning regimen included straightening thousands of tiny curls, applying false eyelashes, and a tremendous amount of makeup. Before that day I knew she was beautiful, but on the surface she had altered her appearance so drastically because she wanted us to admire her. She had decided that she loved the way people looked at her in disguise, and it was worth the daily cost of a two-hour commitment to sell the image she wanted to create. Don't get me wrong; I'm not saying any of that is bad. I am using her choices as an illustration. Her attention to weight, grooming, and appearance showed incredible dedication. But they also helped me know that without those things, she would have been less happy.

Reflections in the Mirror Assessment

Which version of yourself do you most often present? I've created a list of words that describe what people see when they look in the mirror.

- Which do you identify with?
- Feel free to circle the words that connect or keep the list in your head for privacy's sake.
- Do they describe the way you want others to see you?

- That's important for the next part of our discussion.
- Be honest with yourself about the words you don't like, as well as the words you enjoy hearing or wish others might say about you.

Handsome	Oily	Acne
Beautiful	Old	Guilty
Homely	Youthful	Ashamed
Ugly	Tired	Liar
Sad	Weak	Tough
Happy	Exhausted	Cold
Angry	Confident	Unlovable
Melancholy	Glowing	Lovely
Kind	Gruff	Fake
Sweet	Hesitant	Warm
Generous	Shy	Hateful
Rugged	Calm	Hurt
Rough	Flirtatious	Dirty
Wrinkled	Funny	Gorgeous

Now look at the list through the eyes of others.

- What words would others use to describe you?

- If you're brave, you'll ask.
- How do you feel about that?
- There's no right or wrong, just an honest list.

I recently encountered a word in my belief system that really troubled me. For years I had been lovingly called an energizer bunny. Admittedly I'm an overachiever, but my friends have told me that I'm kind, a hard worker, a good cook, a leader, smart, and even wise. So you can imagine why bells and whistles went off inside my head. When I examined this word and acknowledged just how deeply it was rooted inside my heart, I grew in disdain. I hated the moment I had to admit it was controlling how my scales tipped. What is my word? Wounded.

Being wounded shows up in really awful places in the mirror. It is bags underneath both eyes, a little extra weight, a frown, sad eyes, or disappointment staring right back from inside the mirror. Words like worthless, rejection, misunderstood, invisible, unwanted, unloved, unlovable, disrespected, distrusted, devalued, disconnected, taken advantage of, foolish, inadequate, guilty, shameful, and betrayal are words that bubbled up when considering my own mirror. As I stood there I questioned what had transpired, causing me to spotlight each negative belief I held.

Arriving at the answer was not an easy task, but it was clear that I had a significance problem. I had put the incorrect value onto the wrong things. I had carried unforgiveness from painful experiences for years. Self-inflicted pain and shame had slipped in undetected as I had not forgiven myself for past offenses, and I had given away permission to far too many people for way too long. Unwittingly, dozens of people had been allowed to have unrealistic expectations of me. I had let some of them down. I had allowed others to wear me down, use up my energy, and have time I didn't have left in my schedule to give. I was experiencing caregiver burnout in my job. I had harbored abuse and emotional abandonment memories, and I had allowed dysfunctional relationships in my life to cross unnecessary boundaries. I was operating so far outside of my wheelhouse that I missed more opportunities than I was comfortable with. As a natural achiever, I let myself down, and as a leader, I had let others down. I experienced a vicious cycle of exhaustion, disappointment, and overcommitment that was not just noticeable, it was racing out of control. I had set myself up for the ultimate crash—and when it arrived, I was not prepared.

Why am I sharing this with you? I have met so many people who are carrying the weight of the world on their shoulders and they are crumbling in silence. It's so easy to neglect the time to look into the mirror, inflating the false belief that you can be superman or wonder woman. The world wants you to be invincible, and when you give them what they want, they will just ask for more. All the while your own neglect has opened the back door for brokenness to seep in and your entire identity is replaced by emptiness. And one day the sun comes up, and the person in the mirror is unrecognizable.

When I looked in the mirror I could barely distinguish the person on the other side. The emptiness, pain, confusion, and the weight of the world had consumed every corner of my being. I had put on a good show for some, but I was left with nothing but a shell and a mirror when the edges started crumbling.

As I worked through the list above, I considered what words I had spoken to myself. What messages I had allowed to suck the wind out of my sails. I had to make the same decision you're making today. Is getting rid of this mess worth the effort? I had to start the same journey you're walking. I had to decide the pain I'd been dragging around had weighed me down long enough. And enough was finally enough.

Are you there? Is the mirror sending you a message that your life is out of balance? Are you spinning out of control or on the brink of falling apart? If you could hit the pause button and the world would stop spinning, would you rebalance the scales?

If you said yes, stay with me. We'll get through this journey together. Based on what I know, it will be worth it. Obviously there are no guarantees in life, but if you're willing to take the risk, embrace the journey, and choose a better future, there is hope ahead.

Journaling Opportunity:

- Draw a mask. Decorate it.
- What things are you placing behind the masks you wear for different people?
- Write those words around the mask on your page.
- Now draw a mirror. Make it large enough to write words on.
- What words identify the way you see yourself in the mirror?

- How is God's view of you different than your own view?
- What might His word choices be?

10

cover-up

"That's the kind of people the Father is out looking for: those who are simply and honestly themselves before him in their worship" (John 4:23, MSG).

THE NEXT GIFT in your symbolic box is a caution sign. You know, the yellow diamond with a symbol directing you to lean on your fear mechanism and avoid danger ahead?

Have you ever had a flat tire or engine trouble? You step out of the vehicle staring at this inconvenient truth. The solution is going to take time and probably resources you don't currently have at your disposal. Calling a tow company or a mechanic always has dollar signs attached to the untimely experience. A quick fix would be helpful in moments like this, and the wrong fix can be disastrous.

Just when you thought we were getting to the end of this forgiveness journey, another element has surfaced that we need to address. You may know it as denial, but for this conversation we're going to call it a cover-up, and you should be warned, it is incredibly dangerous. The worst part is that it looks innocent. It happens at that moment you avoid confrontation, you bend and let your values be ignored, or you sit quietly when your feelings are hurt. The damage happened at the hand of someone else, but it is your lack of response that actually created the problem. In this time, you need to learn to forgive yourself as much as you forgive others. And it is critical that you willingly shine the spotlight on it and face reality. Covering a problem up is not the same as fixing it.

You likely picked up this book because there are people in your life whose failures you have carried around with you. This chapter is not about them, and I would like you to pack them up inside the box and leave them there for a few minutes. Today is about you. Let's begin by asking a very direct question: Do I need to forgive myself?

You may be one of the many people who find it easy to forgive others but you beat yourself up. You might encounter moments where you are hard on yourself. This typically shows up in tears of frustration, anger when you lose; unkind words spewed when you have made a mistake, or internalized pain when you are critiqued. While these responses may be natural, they are not helping you grow or gain control of your life. So in moments where they are exposed you may do absolutely anything in your power to cover them up.

There is a reason I used the word cover-up. Okay, I know that's two words, but stick with me. I have covered up how I felt, and I bet you have too. Over and over I was compelled to hide how people thought I would/should respond. Some even told me to suppress my feelings, to go back to life, and to suck it up. Like many of you, I withheld emotion, pain, anger, hurt, exhaustion, stress, and years' worth of residual feelings left behind by other people and their baggage. I was pretty good at avoiding the truth about how I felt when they treated me that way.

One of the worst memories I have connected to my sexual abuse was the moment I chose to be bold, to find courage, and to tell an adult what was happening to me. Her response was unthinkable: "Go home, and never tell anybody what you just said to me."

Later that same day I ran away from home. Too young to fend for myself, I thankfully ran to a different adult that did listen, had compassion, and helped me process the situation. Everyone needs a person who can help work through the messiness. When there is impending destruction and residual effects, we need someone to help us rebalance the scales. When who you want to be and who others think you are have become distorted, you will need a voice that reminds you the mirror is not broken, even when everything visible is strangely unrecognizable.

I grew up in Colorado, and our family had a hobby. Legend has it, we have been on every dirt road in the state. The fable might actually be true. Our jeep was a well-loved member of the family. Picture with me a steep mountain road, just wide enough for one vehicle to travel. It's beautiful in this setting, with trees all around and a little drop-off to the right. It's a sunny day, as are most days in Colorado. Take a breath of clean mountain air. There's no top or doors on the jeep, so we can all be closer to God's big creation. That's my mom making quiet but bold acknowledgments of the cliff's presence. If she'd open her eyes, she would realize just how beautiful the view is, 100 feet below. She's holding anything she can find while air rushes through her teeth. My dad is the wide-eyed one steering and smiling from ear to ear. He's taking in every leaf, stone, and water droplet nature provided. He's in love with the entire scenario, and she's more than a little concerned. When I say they are not on the same wavelength, it's an understatement.

Now picture the brilliant yellow sign ahead on the right. It has a mountain drawn on one side and jagged edges with falling rocks on the other. If you have ever driven in the mountains you may have seen one. Their diamond shape was created to announce impending danger. Which of my parents is paying the most attention to the sign? The driver is the one that must react wisely, yet it's the passenger that seems to understand more clearly as warning pebbles click over the sharp edge, bouncing out of view.

A serious jeep driver carries a jack, a winch, and a significant toolbox with the knowledge that adventure can be paused by misfortune. My dad always had a canteen, matches, a roll of toilet paper, duct tape, and a medical kit under the seat. A jeep is a specialized machine made for such an occasion, but even jeeps fail. An ill-equipped driver could be lost in the wilderness for days. Even a trained driver could turn the wheel wrong or hold the brakes too long and a daring adventure could go south in the blink of an eye.

Hairpin turns and high elevations require serious calculation. Could you imagine if something mechanical broke down on the vehicle just as the road narrowed along the cliff's edge? A problem like that could result in the use of a compass and hiking boots to get help. Clearly a vehicle that close to the edge should not tempt fate.

I'm standing before you with your very own caution sign. Are you driving too close to the edge? Are you speeding for the current conditions? Is your partner alerting you to warning signs? Are you well prepared for the challenges ahead?

I'm reminded of Psalm 23. David, the writer, was a shepherd and later a king. His words, "I walk through the valley of the shadow of death, and I do not fear evil things," catches my breath. He certainly wasn't driving a jeep, but his next words explain the control of his thoughts, "You are with me." God's presence should be so comforting that we are challenged to surrender our fear and control issues to Him. That's a lot to ask, but even the challenge to give it to us is something God can help with.

You need to know that the way may be possible, but it might be dangerous as well. If you think about it, shoving your repressed feelings down inside and never talking about them again, that's like driving the jeep over the edge of the mountain. There is a voice telling you to stop, to be careful, and to avoid the free fall. Let me be your voice of reason, let me take you by the shoulders, look you in the eye, and assure you—that option is not a good one. It will end in the worst kind of way. It may not be right this moment, but down the road, when you're not expecting it … some day, it will creep up and attack. And it will bring destruction.

Another road sign you might encounter is also yellow and diamond shaped. It reads, "Road Closed Ahead." At the moment you begin to reveal the truth to someone you trust, you might discover they are not prepared to receive all of the proverbial Pandora's box you have stored up. That's okay. Share what they can handle and save the rest for another time. Your "stuff" might be a lot to comprehend, so give some grace to the person hearing about your wounds. This is another place a counselor might be a great person to share with. They can guide you with professional wisdom. If you handle this well, the road will open back up and you'll have the opportunity to travel there again. Don't push beyond those established boundaries until they are ready to be opened.

What's all the fuss? Why the caution, you might ask? Is it really all that dangerous to drive near the edge of the cliff? I'm experienced, you might say. I've done this before, or I'm an expert at covering it up, looking the other way, and simply choosing to enjoy the ride.

A jeep driver may carry duct tape, but they know it's for temporary fixes. A vehicle that loses control could go over the edge, and no amount of preparedness can put it back together again. Does that sound familiar? Is your view from the top of the cliff leaning too far over? Are you running up the mountain into uncharted territory? Are you even aware of how little control you have?

Everyone has a different definition of what a cliff looks like. But driving along the edge of the cliff must be an occasional experience. Don't hang out there too long. If you realize something could go wrong, don't cover it up. The answer is STOP, put on the emergency brake, and begin assessing the situation. The real problem is often quite obvious, but sometimes its presence has been ignored because the view is so beautiful or the journey is filled with so much fun.

Attached to that adventure may be a lot of baggage, a lot of emotions, or evidence of past violations of yourself. How long have you been ignoring emotional warning signs? Have you just been covering up the truth of the situation for too long? One giant clue could be anger and resentment that you've ignored too long. There is a point where all of that stuffed inside emotion comes blowing out from undercover. And when it does, a seemingly happy and together person experiences burnout, mental breakdown, or suicidal thoughts.

Pause for a minute while I help you understand something. You might think burnout is just exhaustion or that it is just a small problem. But if you encounter burnout, you'll discover it to be a chaotic mix of depression, anxiety, fear, and all of the mess of life landing right in your lap at the same time. All of the emotions you have compressed and avoided have come back for an unexpected visit. That experience may be the biggest nightmare you'll ever encounter.

So how do you get there? The answer is not surprising—it's a mixture of unforgiveness, violated boundaries, and avoidance. It came about by you trying to make peace, being the nice guy, stepping back, and letting others run all over you. It happened when you avoided conflict. It happened when you took criticism too personally and when you didn't speak up for yourself.

People who care about you will share their concerns, and you may need to learn to have an open dialogue that doesn't leave you wounded. If you fit that description, tell someone. Allow them to help you first with gentle critique, then more direction, and eventually full-blown accountability. It's a tender process.

If you are a person who doesn't get wounded by sensitivity, be conscious of the fact that many of your friends and family members do. This is a great place for you to be a good friend and help them overcome that challenge. Be sensitive to their needs.

Let's consider the things you have glossed over in your world. Which of these actions have you inflicted upon yourself? How have they added to your wounded persona? Have you ever nursed those wounds or felt sorry for yourself? Have you ever used those wounds as an excuse to enjoy the pain a little bit?

Have you ever thought you needed to forget past offenses that were done to you but instead they came back in your dreams, in your fears, or in your anxious moments? Consider that your oversensitivity or your lack of sensitivity may be fueled by your desire to let go of the past, but it's just not working.

Now let's consider everyone that has ever hurt you—all of them, each individually and together collectively—no matter how old you are, many people have hurt you over time. There is absolutely no way you could ever undo all you have experienced, and the great news is, you have become who you are today because of all of the negative things you've experienced in life. You are stronger because of the things you've survived. Don't view that as less significant than it is.

In the moments you are awake (about 57,000 seconds each day), you experience ongoing life. That life doesn't slow down or speed up, but you can pack it so full that it begins to add to your weight, and the stress can become overwhelming. Put that together with the baggage you've already put on your scale and soon you may wonder if you are out of balance. Remember, three things have to be in balance at all times—who you are, who you want to be, and who others think you are.

You have expectations about how your life should function, and when those expectations come to a halt because of someone else's intrusion or demands, you have choices to make. How will you respond? The typical person has a set of rules they have created for themselves called boundaries, and those boundaries determine how you will react. Go back to that scale and consider how you respond when things don't go as planned. How do they go when they are not done to your liking or up to your level of expectation? How do you express or repress your feelings?

We have all encountered a person (or more than one) that has removed our ability to respond properly. They shut us down, they physically hurt us, they manipulate the situation, or they cast blame. Those people may need us to create bigger boundaries, they may need us to end our relationship, or they may need us to intervene with their behaviors. The very person who has caused pain may be the one who needs forgiveness the most. And that is far from a simple endeavor.

In all of those situations, you will respond by taking on pain, either physically, mentally, or emotionally. You will carry that pain until you decide to let it go. For some, that "letting-go" process happens immediately, but in other situations, it is longer lasting. The key is finding the right time to let it go. That doesn't happen by accident. You've got to be in the practice of letting go.

Go back to the vicious cycle chart. Are you in the habit of ending the cycle, converting it to a new format, or are you just covering it up? Are you handling it directly, or are you in denial of its existence? Covering up past, present, or future mistakes won't allow you to heal. Letting go should happen in small increments that you can manage (with wise counsel if needed).

Here are the steps of letting go:

1. Choose the right person to help you work through your covered-up experience.
2. Decide you will expose the truth.
3. Make sure you have forgiven yourself for your contribution.
4. Verbalize the need to see change happen.

It's not like taking out the trash or doing the laundry; it's a task that must be done with care. Removing what has been covered up may be painful, but it's the beginning of a very important journey. In the end, that beautiful person you want to see in the mirror will find balance in the way you experience life. The goal is to uncover who you are, who you want to be, and who others think you are in a much healthier way.

Journaling Opportunity

Draw a caution sign.

- What warnings are you aware of in your life?
- What have you covered up?
- What edges of life are you running up against while ignoring the warning signs?

- Is it better to live on the edge or to choose the safer route?
- Do you need to share your story or find a therapist that can help you out?
- Make the call, don't put it off—there's no time like the present to commit to a new pattern of living.

11

the badge of pain

"If you can't fly, then run.
If you can't run, then walk.
If you can't walk, then crawl.
But by all means, keep moving."
—Martin Luther King Jr.

IT'S CHAPTER 11, and now that you are an expert imagineer, the challenge has arrived for you to experience another item from the box. Carefully select the beautiful shiny star in front of you. Badges alert people to the identity and credentials of the wearer. Go ahead and put your badge on your shirt, buckle up, and get ready for the next conversation.

When a triathlete is training for the big event, they can't let a little discomfort get to them. It's a beautiful sight to see hundreds of long-distance runners take off in search of affirmation earned by their goals. They would be unable to win if they stopped for every twinging muscle or aching joint, but because the brain is wired to disregard negative distraction, a person who is slightly hurt is able to ignore the pain and press onward. Great athletes are praised for this type of endurance. The secret to their success is that they train and condition for their work.

It's hard to train for a crisis in life, but being prepared for future obstacles is a great skill to have. The way we learn to maneuver a crisis is practice. Successfully staying on track during a crisis can be an eye-opening experience, and it can strengthen you for the future. There will no doubt be more crisis moments to come. That's part of being human.

To an individual who has run a very difficult course of life's challenges, pain may be just as severe as it is for the athlete. It's just a different type of pain. If you're a person who has persistent aching emotional tenderness, you may be the most susceptible to prolonged challenges. If you're the individual who seems to always have it together, who helps everyone else out, or who notices when others are struggling, you may be just as prone to emotional injury, but you may not be prepared for the moment things break down.

In Japan, there is a phrase, "Death of a thousand paper cuts." The meaning of the phrase has changed dramatically over the centuries, but the sting within the words shouts with pain. The debilitating feeling created by this tiny infliction seems overrated, but somehow it's not. Imagine a number so large that it would cause death. Now step back and assess just how many paper cuts at one time would be survivable? Your story may not be as dramatic as mine, but if you're a person with a list of small moments of unforgiveness woven throughout life, the path is potentially the same. The problem with many tiny wounds is that they pile up. Unattended issues tied to emotional strength can be draining and even life-threatening.

Persistent pain gets tucked away, like a jack-in-the-box, ready to pop up at the most inopportune times—usually way down the road when we least expect it. But have you discovered that you kind of like the chaos that's created inside that pain?

Have you ever shaken a soft drink up just to see it explode when the pressure is released? That's the kind of explosion that can occur when all of the elements are lined up and you've stuffed your emotions inside for too long. You pushed them down, ignored their presence, and covered them up until one day—*boom!*

There's a less beautiful picture that tends to be shunned from our mind—you know the one—it is suppressed reality. What is that reality? It looks something like bulky shackles confining every movement. It happens when pain is carried around and secretly worn as a badge of courage. We drag it around like it's a part of our identity and we buy into the lie that it's needed to exist. If we have been victimized enough, we don't know how to do life without those motivational memories.

Before you dismiss the personal connection here, take a moment to think about what you have suppressed. Have you been secretly hiding pain so others won't know it's there? Do you fear feeling weak? Do you hide things out of shame? Whose shaming words are you afraid of most?

Or are you the opposite? Do you go around blowing up all over people right out in plain sight, dropping angry salutations at those sharing the road with you? Do you share negative talk with coworkers, fixating on the worst-case scenario over coffee or a beer? Do your kids stay clear of you when you are in "a mood?" None of these scenarios are good, but they stem from the same point of origin.

Even worse, the pain we have identified is waiting for the worst moments to explode like the can of soda, spewing out and touching way more than ever intended. Not only is it hard to clean up, but it's also impossible to remove all the mess you've left behind. Beyond the initial mess are the guilt and shame following those actions. The force of your eruptions causes damage beyond your reach and control.

Out of fear of explosive rage, you may be the person who takes your pain and punishes yourself instead. You own it, coddle it, and want control, and that's the only way to go about it. Hiding it right under the surface works. After all, who would you be without that part of your story? You are a survivor, and survivors get props for … well—surviving. What helped you make it through the unthinkable is the same thing that made you tough, and what made you tough makes you successful.

Our culture seems to aid this model of behavior by saying things like: "Healthy people don't have messy lives." They don't blow up or show their baggage in public places, right? First John 1:9 challenges us to give our messiness to God and allow Him to forgive us. What a beautifully opposite cultural experience! Can you imagine if each time you confess a failure it was forgiven by the God of the universe? It's really that simple. And it is incredibly humbling!

The world loves a good comeback story. Television and movies are made of people who had all of the elements to fall apart, but through some miracle they held it together. Their triumph story makes the world believe that if we endure long enough, are tough enough, or have enough gumption—then we could become winners. So we try, but a lot of times that means we hide the root of the problem. When we ask God to get involved, it may seem too simple, but His forgiveness is readily available. Are you willing to ask?

There's a very dark side that is revealed by those who hide their pain too long. When it's convenient, the suffering individual reaches inside, takes out their pain, and uses it for show-and-tell. Sometimes people even think it's amazing because we (the survivors) have made it through something really difficult. But don't leave it out. You don't really want someone to see the whole truth, just the part that gets noticed. Right?

Journaling Opportunity

- Think about how you carry your pain. If you could draw a picture of the relationship you have with the pain in your life, what would it look like?
- Are you the soda can, the stuffed-down angry person, or the just-below-the-surface pain hoarder?
- Do any of these resonate?
- Maybe you can identify your pain with another analogy. What I know for sure is that pain that is mishandled can become your sharpest weapon—for others or yourself.

Take a moment and picture your pain, wounds, unforgiven experiences, trashed boundaries, resentment, and dysfunction. What does all that baggage look like? Is it zipped up in a backpack that you sling over your shoulder and carry around? Is it hooked to you by a chain that is dragging you down? Is it tucked inside your pocket like a treasure waiting to be reexamined? Are you wearing it like your favorite T-shirt? It doesn't matter how you transport it. The fact is there is weight in its very existence. Your pain is bound to you, or worse, it's consuming you. That pain does more than define your choices; it defines who you think you need to be. Pain can become you—everything about you.

In the very worst moments that pain gets unpacked like an overfilled suitcase in the cartoons. First the zipper begins to move, and suddenly the stuff inside flings everywhere. When unforgiveness is not handled correctly it finds its way into the heart, mouth, or physical actions. In front of us, we watch helplessly as it destroys things we've worked hard to put in place. The choice to harbor unforgiveness has the power to inflict copious amounts of pain directed back at us, at a friend, a stranger, or someone we love.

Have you ever experienced an outburst hangover? It typically comes after using the pain factor as a grenade launcher filled with missiles directed at the ones we care about the most. It's that remorseful experience when you know your lack of self-control ruined something—or everything. It's the moment the switch in your brain realizes the damage and turns on a new emotion—self-pity.

Researchers have uncovered evidence showing that a large number of pain carriers repeat the cycle. In fact, when adding up the possibilities, most victims act out or inflict pain in scenarios much like their own. Internet sources provide straightforward numbers. 33 percent of abusers abuse someone else (Cambridge.org); 20 percent of neglected people neglect others (healthychildren.org); 92 percent of most individuals have lied to save face (*WA Post*); 57 percent of abandoned kids abandon another relationship in life; and nearly all who are bullied will bully someone else in time. When you read these statistics and don't see yourself listed—DO NOT let yourself off the hook. Contemplate what types of pain you have encountered and what type you have dished out to others. Wounded people wound others—plain and simple.

The most obvious form of unfiltered forgiveness is present in the act of sabotage. People who intentionally ruin events, relationships, conversations, jobs, possibilities, or rehab programs have a lot of buried pain.

Chaotic situations are among the most interesting places some people thrive. Have you ever noticed that when the chaos settles, there's a problem? If quiet seems like too much, deep thinking becomes an obsessive thought zone. Insecurity leads to bad self-talk, and then you are walking into the extreme danger zone where some of those stuffed-down feelings begin slipping out of control. The classic sabotage expert has discovered that in order to cover up their presence, it's better to create a smokescreen and divert attention. That attention comes with a cost. And when you feel yourself tipping into that space, be careful—very careful.

When a person is unwilling to sit with who they are and consider what makes their own image unwelcomed, they will lob a sabotage bomb out into the world and wait to see what happens. The goal is to make another person show they care, they love, or they are committed. It's a type of test—and it might be as destructive as the soda can explosion. The person doing the sabotage doesn't really mean to make such a big deal out of it, but they do. And sometimes it backfires, and whoever is on the receiving end gets fed up, tired, angry, or ready to quit. Every single day relationships end over petty sabotage, which is caused by insecurity. That doesn't make much sense, and psychologists everywhere are retained to meet with clients who need to work through these patterns. For every person that asks for help, there are many more unwilling to ask.

Not everyone pokes at circumstances to test their stability, so there must be another way to allow unforgiveness to take over. There is, and it's called revenge. It's a little self-righteous, and it's a lot destructive.

Revenge is actually a type of sabotage that feels like it's deserved. Feeling that getting back, having the last word, evening up the score, or proving your point can be justified can be quite harmful to your sense of direction. The attention, energy, and satisfaction that are the driving factors are simply misguided. Revenge will not ever make you feel better. Revenge won't solve the problem. And the deeper issue is that revenge requires a relentless amount of negative energy to stay fueled. All that energy has to come from somewhere. So while the mind is fixated on getting back, housekeeping is being neglected. I'm not talking about cleaning your bathroom; I'm talking about the parts of your inner core that need to be kept in check. Revenge can include diminished self-care. It can include weeks of missing work or appointments, neglected commitments, or even a lack of eating, all the while diverting energy toward the revenge source as a key function of life. It sounds pretty misguided when it's broken down so simplistically. And it is at the very central point a horrible way to go about life.

Another horrible option is remaining in a volatile relationship where neither side is willing to forgive. When two bomb droppers, missile throwers, revenge seekers, soda can shakers, emotion stuffers, or wound

coddlers are in a relationship together, the future is pretty grim. It's hard to see how all of the passion that once held the relationship together can fizzle up and be gone. In fact, it's not gone; it's transformed and it's hate-filled. When those two broken people found each other, the energy to be vengeful drew them closer, but that quickly changed to patterns that destroy both of them and those around them.

If these negatively charged magnets fuel one another, vengeance becomes the game. People who were once incapable of any unkindness begin to entertain the most hateful thoughts and actions if they are provoked. If you're in this zone, there is so much more that we could talk about. Letting go may seem 100 percent impossible, but I assure you, even someone who is stuck in this web of living can experience the gift of forgiveness. It won't come easy, and it won't be accidentally stumbled upon. It is going to take some hard work and determination, but it will pay off.

One of the most dangerous driving conditions is fog. Turn on your headlights and you still can't see. Turn on your brights and the beams just bounce back. Slow, steady, careful attention must be used at this moment. Other vehicles, trees, ditches, even cliffs might be lurking in the

cloudiness. Nothing can prepare you for the experience except focus and familiarity with the terrain. The more you learn to walk in healthy pathways, the more familiar they will become. The road may not be obvious; there may be pitfalls. You must pay attention, and you must notify any uncertain obstacles before it's too late. Countless scenarios show us the dangers that unresolved issues can cause. There is only one pathway out of that fog. That path is lined with forgiveness, grace, and understanding.

Letting go of something someone has done is hard. Forgiveness takes intention and commitment. The decision to forgive may seem like the furthest thing from your mind, but if you can muster up the courage to just try it, I'm confident that you will see how life-altering this gift can be.

This is the moment you've been waiting for. It's the challenge to let it go. I am positive that you can do it, and I am positive it will be hard. But it is a choice. Freedom from all that weighs you down starts here. It's not about waiting until the end of the book or for a better day, and today is the day to start the process.

If you are reading to help someone else, if there is a vengeance seeker in your inner circle, you have the ability to aid them in the healing process.

The words you say, the boundaries you set, and the encouragement you offer for wise decision-making are the answers to keeping this train on the tracks. Influence, support systems, and accountability are highly important.

If you're a parent trying to figure out your role in this, stay strong. They need you. If your child calls you every time they get in a fight with a friend, a spouse, or a coworker, you have influence. But your job is not to solve their problems or to save them from their own destructive tendencies. Your job is to support. Preaching at them, fixing it for them, shaming, or feeding the fire of negative thinking is not helping this person head in the right direction. Here are nine keys for the support role relationship.

1. Remind them what is most important in the big picture of life. Likely the situation they are fixated upon is so big and so consuming that another view is hard to see, and may even be small in focus.
2. Stay the course. Don't give up. Don't quit because this person is not getting it right. They need you to help them find the truth. They need you to steer the train for a bit, even if it feels like the

train is out of control. But ask permission to help, and only help if things are headed in the right direction.

3. Never join this individual on the journey down the wrong path. Self-medication, obsession, destructive thinking, and self-harm is never the answer. Don't support those ideals.
4. Be you. You've built this relationship; don't let it change around the situation at hand. You need to be able to stand firm and still be there at the end of the challenge. Be you, and remember to be faithful and loyal to the relationship.
5. If you have the choice to support or not, choose support. That may be exhausting. It may be overwhelming—but choose to be supportive with the amount of energy you have. Do not become overwhelmed by helping a friend. You can't carry their weight, nor should you. But you can be the best friend/relative they need at the moment.
6. Don't add to the problem. I've seen in-laws fuel the fire, friends dig the ditch deeper, and family members go to bat in all the wrong places. If you wonder if you're making the problem worse, stop

and think about what the consequences of your actions might be. Choose wisely.

7. Speak wisdom into the situation. If they ask your opinion, add wisdom, insight, and value to the conversation. That's not gossip, that's not shame, that's not intimidation. That's truth, kindness, and providing tools for them to make good decisions.
8. Realize they need time. Give it to them. But not too much time. Be emotionally tuned in so you know when to step up and ask if they need your help.
9. And sometimes your role is silence. You can't fix it, you can't live it for them, and you can't change their mind. So if you have nothing wise to add, wait to be asked before speaking.

If you are in one of those relationships, stand strong, be wise, and be willing to continuously point the momentum in a positive direction. Keep pointing—it may take a while.

Wearing pain as a badge of honor is not becoming of anyone. If your identity has become one of a victim, it's time for a change. It's time to lay down the load and get rid of it. It's weighing you down, changing you into a person you don't want to be, and possibly ruining the other relationships in your life.

Take off the badge, lay it down, and choose freedom—there's something I can't explain about this decision. Until you've had the experience, you won't get it. But once you understand freedom from the chains that tie you down because of unforgiveness, anger, vengeance, and dysfunctional living, you will want to spread the message to the world. Once you do, you will be free.

Journaling Opportunity

I thought this might be a good place for you to stop and contemplate what we just talked about. Letting go takes a lot of energy and the reward is huge, but you didn't get to this place without a lot of layers. So let's peel back some layers and consider what matters most.

Contemplative thought is a time when you sit alone with your thoughts and consider their implications. Even if you haven't journaled in the other chapters, I'd like for you to commit to this exercise. I would encourage you to get some paper and answer these questions in writing. You may want to journal about each independently or address them all at once.

One great opportunity is to take an extended amount of time and just sit silently. Ask God to show you how He is working in this journey. How is His forgiveness something you need, want, or fear?

Emotions may find their way into this experience. That's okay. The energy you have put into receiving and carrying this pain may bring out tears or even anger. It's all a part of the process.

Here's a crazy question to consider:

What if you never stuffed feelings in the first place? Can you imagine that?

Now think about this:

What if you never experienced this particular pain and it never existed? Would life be better? How?

A few more deep thoughts:

How do you typically respond in the face of pain? Your response is what is in question here. How do you respond when things go wrong? What happens when you aren't smack-dab in the middle of pain?

Going even deeper:

What destructive habits have you formed? If you could change those habits, what would you rather do instead? You can ponder the feeling when you know there are better solutions than you typically make. Is it possible that you could break the cycle?

What about the future? If you put this book down, walk away, and nothing changes, could that be okay? We can become victims reliving our past all too often or creating new victims because of our own dysfunction. What concerns you the most about those concepts?

I can't say this boldly enough: In your life—for you to experience the gift of forgiveness, the cycle of woundedness must stop. Simply asking yourself if you want it to stop is not enough action to make it less painful. You actually have to commit to the process of healing. If you are willing to allow God to be the most significant part of the process, this healing will have an even greater result.

If you're reading this book because you know someone that is not just stuck in a cycle; they are delusional about the very existence of its existence. Even if you picked the book up so you could help a friend, I wonder what is here for you to apply to your own life. Is anything striking a chord?

If you're reading this book for yourself, consider how your support system can help you. Could you ask people to help you differently than they do now? Could you have an honest conversation that would set you up for a better potential of moving forward? What's holding you back?

We can keep asking questions or we can get active with results. Your action is needed for things to change. I've found that asking questions is a good way to think about what has to happen, but not all questions are created equally. Sometimes asking someone you trust will help you process the things you struggle to see.

If you've been asking questions for a long time and you aren't getting the answers you want, change the question. "What's wrong with me?" could be changed to, "What am I seeing wrong?" or, "Why do I let that bother me?" could be changed to, "What is bothering me?" Practice reframing your questions and look for the right answers. Look from more than one perspective to see if you're asking the right questions.

When you start asking the right questions, you'll see the answers you were looking for all along. That's when you truly begin the forgiveness process.

12

round and round and round again

"Without forgiveness, life is governed by … an endless cycle of resentment and retaliation."

—Roberto Assagioli

REMEMBER THE SUNNIEST day of your childhood. Did you ever experiment with a magnifying glass? The next symbol in the made-up gift box is a magnifying glass. You'll need it to take a closer look as we complete the map, which focuses on the cycles of pain, decision-making, and response in your life. Take notice of the good habits you have but particularly focus on the not-so-good habits as we work through the next few pages. Let's examine the details and see if there are patterns that can be identified or strengthened.

In your mind, I'd like you to draw a circle. Fill it with every wrong thing any individual person has ever done toward you. Put the smallest incidents on the edges of the circle and the huge ones in the middle. Think of the circle like a magnifying glass. Take a close look at all of this garbage. It has at some point inflicted pain in your life. Some of that pain has taught you great wisdom. Some of that pain has swept you off your feet.

I used to teach high school science. Students would look through the microscope to attempt to draw and label what they saw through the magnifying lenses. Each year a new crop of students needed to be taught to draw perfect circles, use the right magnification, and draw things they had never seen before. And each year at least one student would tighten their microscope lens down on an air bubble, draw the wrong thing, and then roll their eyes when I made them redraw the specimen. You can't properly label the parts of an air bubble using biology terms.

Last summer I used the same concept with a group of preschoolers, but this time I gave them a magnifying glass. The simplicity of the project made it a wonderful experience. I have to say, phrases like, "Look at the way this bug gloops along," and, "Mr. Ant sure is strong," are the types of observations that make a teacher's heart jump with joy.

There is more to this observation than a picture of ants marching in formation, flexing their muscles with your picnic lunch. Sometimes you simply need a magnifying glass to see the obvious. Sometimes you look too closely at a problem and you overanalyze it, or you analyze the wrong thing completely.

I'm placing a simple magnifying glass in your hand. I don't want to get too complicated. Just say what you really see, what you truly feel, and don't even worry if you have to make up words to describe it. Observation can create perspective, and perspective can be enlightening, even when things appear to be normal.

As we draw the circles of your life together, you'll be excited to see that some of your observations are breathtakingly wonderful. You may also notice that some of the things you label are not what you'd like to see. I'm going to predict some repetitive behaviors in your life. When you notice them, label them. Call them what they are. Then progress each one forward as it manifests in your life. Before you know it, evidence will appear, and your observations will help you to define the problem(s) simply. My hope is that this exercise will help you to see why it influences you so much.

Let me show you how.

Draw that observation circle, just like a magnifying glass and illustrate a specific problem you want to fix.

1. Label each item that has piled up in the center of your lens.
2. Now pick the one that has unforgiveness spilling out from the edges.
3. Label the person's name associated with the image (or a nickname if you don't want them to see this chart).
4. Label details of the situation you remember most dramatically.
5. What good memories did you have that day?
6. Acknowledge any painful memories you have that day (or another period of time).
7. Can you observe the breaking point—where the experience turned from good to bad?
8. Can you identify the issue that repeats in this relationship?
9. What questions should you ask yourself? How did you respond in this instance?
10. Is there a pattern with this person or behavior? What is it?

11. What words most realistically describe this painful situation?

Observation is a skill we learn *before* elementary school, and we hone those skills as we mature. You may need to draw several circles to see the entire problem. And like every other person in the world, you've likely got more than one problem going at any given time. Your response is what will change as you begin to observe the details.

- o As you magnify the view, was there an observation worth noting?
- o Did you report all you saw, or did you get sidetracked by the wrong items?
- o Did anything surprise you?
- o Were you brutally honest?
- o Was there one memory or incident that you didn't want to examine?
- o What do you have to lose by addressing the issues diagrammed here?
- o Is it possible that the person attached to the situations you have analyzed repeats their behaviors?

- o Has a similar situation ever occurred with another individual?
- o Are you exhibiting any of these same behaviors?

If the answer is yes to any of these questions, then there is a cycle that needs to be broken.

If the answer is no, consider that there is still a cycle, but the issues are not so obvious.

It may be that you are inflicting pain on yourself, that you're secretly punishing yourself by growing in resentment, anger, or self-harm. Numbing yourself is self-inflicted pain too.

The purpose of this conversation is not an end in itself. Don't get stuck here, and please don't stop moving forward. If you're unable to identify any part of the cycle, I don't want you to get frustrated and give up. The purpose of this book is forward momentum. Let's keep moving.

This is not a comprehensive list of pain issues, but a quick list created to help you ponder what steps might be in your story. When you consider the labels for your pain, here are some cyclical issues or specific labels that might stand out:

Sexual abuse

Physical abuse

Arguing

Manipulation

Screaming

Substance misuse

Laziness

Ignoring

Hateful words/angry outbursts

Unwillingness to help out/contribute

Abandonment

Head games

Social media manipulation/bullying

Bullying

Withholding money that is owed

Guilt trips

Passive-aggressiveness

Cheating

Gaslighting

Temper tantrums

Bomb dropping (waiting for the right moment and sabotaging the experience)

Refusing to communicate

Rehashing the past in new ways

Entitlement

Withholding affection to get their way

Selfishness

Overstated/underestimated self-worth

Inflexible

Demanding

Feeling cheated

Angry responses

Taking the easy road

Self-absorption

Self-Inflicted Cycles or Reactions

Please note, these are present in repetition, not single events.

Suicidal ideation

Substance abuse

Cutting

Obsessive picking

Nail-biting

Obsessive body-altering for endorphin release

Screaming/yelling

Idle threats

Food obsession

Tuning important things out

Choosing to treat others wrongly

Burning/cutting/hair pulling

There may be more; feel free to list yours here:

As you write, you may discover an emotional response. Here's a great verse from Psalms to consider as you process these thoughts:

> "If your heart is broken, you'll find God right there; if you're kicked in the gut, he'll help you catch your breath" (Psalm 34:18, MSG).

The more we observe, the more we notice, and the more we notice, the more we have to admit when things don't look right. Keep looking, and practice looking more often. Don't let the issues pile up before you take notice.

Persistence is the key to finding healing in your life. Lots of people talk about the dysfunctional cycles that cause pain, but few people know how to stop them. First, you've got to commit to change. You have got to be willing to do the work and to be ready to face the hard challenges you've lived through, and weigh their value appropriately.

Another key lesson I have taught in school is that energy cannot be created or destroyed. Energy is either chemical, potential, or kinetic. Potential energy is just that—it's potential; it has possibility. It is stored up and ready to use at just the right moment. Kinetic energy is the energy of movement. When something is in motion, it's using kinetic energy. When you consider where you are at this moment, do you think you are standing still, considering movement, or are you ready to get started? You see, there is great news in potential energy and even better news when you're ready to move.

Who is in the way of your happiness? What is stopping your forward movement? What is keeping you from addressing the problem? What excuses have you leaned on which have allowed you to stay in the cycle of pain? How much are you willing to give up to walk away free from it? What will be the reward for standing up against the pain, changing direction, and gaining control of your past, present, and future?

Let's just have a side conversation here: If you're moving, I want to be sure it's in the right direction. Moving backward or moving against what is best for you is counterproductive, and it's not okay. I want to look you in the eye and with the gentlest conversation and nudge you in the right direction. The chains of pain can no longer be given the power to drag you down. If you haven't stopped allowing them to reduce your momentum or stop your energy from moving you in the right direction—today is the day to turn it all around.

Did I mention that the cycle(s) of dysfunction must stop? I just want to remind you how critical that statement is. If you use logic, it's not hard to see how ignoring them can be like a snowball rolling downhill. You know the image: a little snowball is made, then it begins to roll downhill, and before you know it, it's a life-threatening boulder that has consumed you. Remember the man inside the snowball with his arms and legs sticking out? That could be you tangled in the dysfunction of life. What happens when that snowball of pain is created?

This pain has been debilitating long enough! If you've carried it for a few months, a few years, or a few decades—you've allowed the pain to rob you of the freedom to live life to the fullest.

Let's pause to acknowledge something very important. There's a moment when the pain you're experiencing is very real, excruciating, burning hot, and the wounds may be fresh. If someone hurt you yesterday, you may not be ready to move on today, but at some point, you must move forward. If you recently experienced life-altering distress, it may be too soon to work through this process.

When we talk about forgiveness, breaking cycles of pain, and investing in the future—that takes planning. Your brain is not able to extinguish pain the moment it is inflicted. It's important that you are sure that you are past the point of inflection before you make huge life changes. It's not too early to observe the situation, label the key problems, and identify the individuals who brought this moment about. All forms of healing require a process, and that process takes time. Taking permission back from your offender takes time. This cannot and will not happen overnight. Just like the body, heart and mind, it doesn't work that way.

13

choices and voices

"But sin didn't, and doesn't, have a chance in competition with the aggressive forgiveness we call grace" (Romans 5:20-21, MSG).

I AM NOT a karaoke singer, and in fact, I'm not any kind of singer. Put a microphone in my hand and I'm happy to talk, but singing is not my gig. Have you ever been sitting at a stoplight, the perfect song comes on the radio, nobody is in the car, so you go for it … you turn the dial to the right, and for a brief moment, you really love the lyrics? When our kids were little, we used to have a "roll down the window and sing" song list. Driving down the freeway with the window open and the music loud enough can drown out even the worst of us. And for a moment we feel a spark of freedom that ends with the last lyric.

I'm here to tell you that just like that song, forgiveness can give you that voice you desire. You might want to sing it from the mountaintops or even into the microphone while others are listening. Once you have experienced it, you find it's worth sharing. You won't want to drown it out because you'll have a new kind of voice.

I hope you can wrap your head around the forgiveness principle early in life. Forgiveness has the power to heal, add depth to your relationships, and allow you to move about life freely. Absolutely every person on the planet needs forgiveness at times, and that means we have to be willing to give it as well.

You've got a dial in your head. Imagine it like a volume knob labeled 1-10. To the left is the choice to stay silent and let something bother you, and on the right is the freedom to let it go. It's the same freedom you experience when you turn up the music and belt the words like you recorded the song in a studio. Not every experience you have finds the same space on the dial. That's because some of them are just more connected to your core. What happens if you turn the dial and experience them at a different volume? Some people are better at turning the knob, but it's a skill everyone can learn. In fact, living a lifestyle of high-volume forgiveness is a great tool you can learn.

Romans 5:20-21 says: "All that passing laws against sin did was produce more lawbreakers. But sin didn't, and doesn't, have a chance in competition with the aggressive forgiveness we call *grace*. When it's sin versus grace, grace wins hands down. All sin can do is threaten us with death, and that's the end of it. Grace, because God is putting everything together again through the Messiah, invites us into life—a life that goes on and on and on… (MSG).

Forgiveness can be elusive when we connect it to grace. Sometimes it's easier to help you picture what it doesn't look like so you can understand the view more clearly. For example, you see two toddlers fighting for a toy and realize just how silly their squabble is. A few simple words can settle the battle and the children can move on. We teach kids to live a lifestyle of forgiveness early because it is wise for us to acknowledge the need to be able to give forgiveness early in life.

But the older we get, the easier it is to let our brains go back and think about that moment of pain, hold it, reflect on it, internalize it, and harbor our feelings in a place of bitterness. Resentment is one of the deadliest forces on the planet. It steals joy, peace, understanding, grace, words, time, relationships, and happiness daily. Consider what life could be like if those were never missing from our life.

Do you remember the day your life changed and you began to hold onto your pain in a life-altering way? Not like the toddlers that fought over the toy, or the playground friends that didn't talk for an entire day. I'm talking about when you first let pain have a piece of your freedom.

Late one afternoon I was at home in our suburban neighborhood. I was still in elementary school and I lost the freedom of shameless, guilt-free living that I had come so accustomed to as a child. I entered a room of our home just as I had done hundreds of times before but I left with a pain that stayed with me for decades. I allowed it to wound me for the rest of my childhood, and even today, it shapes who I am. Though I am proud to say that it does not hold me captive any longer, thanks to my own forgiveness journey. That day I experienced sexual assault at the hand of a family member. I was young and I was completely caught off guard. I was forced to do things I never imagined. In the end I was never the same again. Before that day I had no idea sex was even a part of life. I'll admit, I was incredibly naive, and that part of my story was just the beginning of several years of abuse.

Like many people, I didn't just have one sexual assault incident with that person, or the next person that violated me. I was in more than one relationship that crossed the line physically, mentally, and emotionally. More than once I encountered physically, emotionally, and even spiritually abusive situations. When those start in your childhood, there's no way to take on the abusers and win readily. I think that's why our culture hates childhood abuse so much. We realize that innocent children have no idea how to speak up for themselves. But what I realize more than ever, is that those innocent children grow up to be wounded, damaged, imprisoned adults who carry around unfinished business that steals their freedom.

You don't have to experience childhood trauma, abandonment, verbal and emotional abuse, or neglect to find yourself at a crossroads, unable to process your pain. The reality is, we teach kids to say "stop" or "no" or "don't do that," but we never teach them what to do when "I'm sorry" and "I hate you" keep hurting our hearts for years down the road.

If I could hold each child on earth, I would look them in the eye and tell them that some words, actions, and people will hurt them more than others. They won't be able to know which ones ahead of time. I would tell them that some people will leave destruction in their world, but there is hope. They don't have to allow that person to take their happiness, joy, or self-worth during the process. But the most important thing I would tell them is that they are not alone, and other people are hurting too.

That deep, dark space where we shove that pain so it will disappear, never to see the light of day—that place will fail us. It is not foolproof, can't hold our secrets, and when they do slip back out of that space—they will be more painful than when we first put them there.

I wish my story ended with a single sexual assault, but it didn't. More than one family member chose to use my body for the wrong reasons. I spoke up, I told a teacher, I told a trusted family friend, and I told my friend's mom. We teach kids to "say something," but the adults in my life didn't know what to do when I did.

When a friend tells you they have experienced something that doesn't quite seem to make sense, I urge you to ask questions. When a coworker comes to the office with a bruise on their forearm or a black eye, when someone takes a few extra sick days and tells you they just slept those days away—think about what they might NOT be saying. Give them a voice; hand them a microphone so they can speak loud enough to be heard. There's a delicate balance between being nosey or coming up with conspiracy theories about what is going on with people you do life with. In the interest of being a friend, consider asking, "Are you okay?" when they tell you they are a little sad. If they express a single detail of a bad situation, please be ready to ask, "Is there a way I can help?" or help connect them with someone trusted who can. As humans, we need to be better at allowing one another to open up about their situation. We must make safe spaces within our conversation, and we have got to work harder at empowering people to talk.

The guys at the office telling jokes and cutting up might not notice when someone is sitting quietly at their desk, choosing not to participate. The ladies around the watercooler might think it's easier to talk about someone's black eye and not speak with her about the incident that occurred. Coworkers, churchgoers, people at the gym—statistics* say at any given moment someone around you has a secret, they have pain, and they have something so big they don't want you to know. Who is in the room with you right now? What permission have you given them to share their pain?

You want your pain to go away and so do the other people you meet. But remember—that pain comes in cycles. And if we don't manage the pain correctly and talk through it, support one another, and give each other courage to face it—we are guilty of perpetuating it.

When someone asks about your pain—speak up. Say it. Let it out. There are cultural rules we have to apply here. Be wise in who and what you say. Find a trustworthy person. Telling a known gossip lover will put you right in the middle of the story sharing your dread. Telling a coworker while you should be focused on work might produce a difficult situation with your boss. Sharing too many details all at once might make a friend overwhelmed and unable to listen to your story. Read the room, but also know that those who care about you care about your pain and past, and can help you heal.

Every story we share has an emotional side and a fact-filled side. Be careful as you express your version of events. When the emotional side takes over, the facts may get twisted or the details muddy. Use words like "it happened like this" to share facts and "it made me feel" to express emotions. Help the listener sort out the difference. And if you're going to share, tell the truth. How you were involved in the situation, if you made it worse, admit it. If you started it, you need to carry some blame, or you are confused by it—speak up. In no way am I saying a victim is to blame, but I also believe that in many situations our reactions can also cause more harm than good.

When you hide your pain, when you choose not to tell others, your mind has a way of filing it away for another day. And just because the situation happened, your brain might not keep all of the details together in a nice, neat file folder. Over time details get distorted. The more traumatic the situation, the more likely the distortion will be.

You may be mad or feel justified in your distress—but if you continue to live in pain, if you hold onto it and choose not to let it go, the people around you will be less likely to listen. This is another important reason for breaking this cycle. If you leave an abusive situation and go right into another one, the friends you have will have a difficult time supporting you. Likewise, if you don't really let it go, you keep dragging it out of the closet and you can't move on—your friends will arrive at a place where they are no longer willing to participate in the journey.

It's time for a gut check. Have you ever shared too much, shared with the wrong person, or withheld details that you shouldn't have? Can you point to those situations and see what pattern they perpetuated in your thinking? Are you able to identify why that won't work in the future?

Therapists, counselors, psychologists, and psychiatrists have a role in our world, and despite your financial limitations, your time constraints, and your fear of breaking open Pandora's box, they can walk this journey with you. Some challenges are beyond the capabilities of your friends. Some experiences need more than a ten-minute talk on the phone. Do you know when to call a therapist? Here are five quick reasons to reach out:

1. I don't have friends to walk this journey with me.
2. I have experienced something that would be considered a crime.
3. I am experiencing fear, anxiety, shame, or extreme feelings because of my pain.
4. I have considered self-harm (on purpose) like cutting, burning, scraping my skin, or I have thought about taking my own life or wished I could die.
5. I don't know what to do, I can't wrap my head around it, and I'm lost.

Of course, there are more reasons to seek help from a professional, like serious weight loss, eating disorders, or experiences that you can't explain to others. This is just a quick list to help you think through the burden of your pain and to consider who might be able to help.

Remember our earlier conversation about permission? Have you given permission to others to take part of you away but you have not received permission to ask for help? Healthy friendships and family members are a two-way street. Nurturing those relationships 365 days a year takes work—lots of work. At times those people will need you to support them, but the beauty of this design is that you will have someone when you need them.

There's a tendency to take the words from someone's mouth and nurture them the wrong way. This is because we listen to respond. Each of us needs to work on listening to hear—hurts, emotions, and what's not being said. When someone shares their pain with you, it's critical that you have established rules for the reaction. Don't give each other permission to harbor or overreact to pain. Be wary of friends that challenge you to fight back, get revenge, or impose pain on someone else. Ask for wisdom, guidance, discernment, and truth from your inner circle, and choose to be someone who brings those same qualities to conversations. Look for solutions that bring growth, forgiveness, grace, mercy, and freedom to the situation.

Journaling Opportunity

Going back to our sound analogy, consider the sound you are making.

- Is it deafening for others to hear?
- Do they turn up the music to drown it out?
- How should the message you're communicating change?

Additionally, think about the voices speaking into your world.

- Are they making your life better or dragging you down?
- What is Jesus' role in your relationships with others?
- Do you have a friend who needs Jesus in order to gain perspective of the messages they send and receive?

The best test of good advice is this simple question: If I listen to this advice, will it improve my future? Is the voice you're looking for going to help you get even or is it going to help you grow stronger? Getting back at someone might feel good at the moment, but it won't improve your future. Hurting someone might relieve pent-up anger, but rage doesn't improve your future. Arguing or proving your point will feel great as you do it, but it's not likely to change someone else's mind. Finally, will that argument really improve your future? You see how this test works. Either it will improve it, or it isn't helpful. Stick with solutions that will. Your future is too valuable to throw away.

The Hope Line

hopeline.com

Pray 9000

pray9000.com

New Life Counselor Network

800-NEW-LIFE

newlife.com

---

* Sources of stats on abusers - page 177

https://www.nsvrc.org/statistics
https://ncadv.org/statistics
https://www.verywellmind.com/the-cycle-of-sexual-abuse-22460

National Dating Abuse Helpline
www.loveisrespect.org

Pathways to Safety International
www.pathwaystosafety.org

National Center for Victims of Crime
www.victimsofcrime.org

Child Abuse Hotline 1-800-4-A-CHILD

National Domestic Violence Hotline 1-800-799-SAFE

14

the cost

"I think a spiritual journey is not so much a journey of discovery. It's a journey of recovery. It's a journey of uncovering your own inner nature. It's already there."

—Billy Corgan

THE COST OF God's forgiveness in our lives was enormous. He gave His only Son, Jesus, in a way that allowed each of us to experience life that we didn't deserve. Choosing to do something wrong is a sin; we know that, but it's hard to fully grasp the fact that each time we do something wrong it should result in the punishment of death being brought upon us. The death penalty would certainly change the way some people drive, the way some people cheat on their taxes, or the way people treat one another. But somehow, because we have been forgiven, even before we have sinned, it is easier to sin again. That doesn't make it right. And I wonder if, deep down, we are confused by the value of our actions.

My best friend and I walked into a store and asked how much a pair of sunglasses cost. I wish you could have seen the moment our eyes locked. We both knew the value of those glasses was more than ten times what we had expected it to be. There was nothing fancy or unique in the initial experience of looking at the glasses inside the case. Even when we had tried them on we had no idea what they would cost. Are you like me? I'm pretty frugal, and I tend to want things for less than they are really worth.

Forgiveness is a commodity that has a sliding value. In some relationships it is worth very little, and in others it is priceless. That may even be the factor that makes a specific relationship worth anything at all. There is certainly a difference in the way we accept forgiveness depending on who is involved. There are times we know it is more genuine. In contrast, if you've been lied to often enough, forgiveness may have no meaning at all.

Today is the day for you to define forgiveness. Who are you going to give it to and in what format will you deliver it? I can't put a set value on forgiveness. It might not look like much inside the glass case, but I can assure you, it's an invaluable item. As proof, I submit this book as my testimonial to prove the importance of the gift of forgiveness.

The day I looked at the sunglasses I had been experiencing severe headaches, made worse by the light. When I considered the price, I refused to make a purchase. The cost simply didn't exceed the value of my pain. In other words, I didn't buy the sunglasses because it was more painful to part with hundreds of dollars than it was to endure the pain for a while more. Are you with me in this analogy? You've got to decide the pain you're carrying is less valuable than the future you have ahead. The price you will pay is hard work and the decision to let go of what you have labeled as valuable.

What is the value of holding onto your abuse, wounds, and pain? What is the cost of letting it go? What work is ahead that will free you from these weights? When you can answer these questions, you're ready to forgive. Sometimes it's simply the decision to move forward that helps us gain the courage to take on these challenges, and that may be all it takes to get started. You may need to come back around and clean up some loose ends if you take the journey too quickly. However, getting rid of some of the weight is better than none of it. Just be sure you are not creating more destruction that others have to clean up. Forgiveness should not be the same messy process that getting to this point was. If you are noticing a messy experience, consider what checks and balances need to be put into place.

We talked about the role of your village in this process. Trust them to help you make decisions that are right, just, and moral. If your decisions are creating more pain, self-destructive behaviors, or causing you to spin out of control, you may need a professional to help you with the next steps. Those decisions are meant to lead you in the right direction.

The day I decided to face my pain, I had to consider: my feelings of abandonment from childhood; physically abusive experiences with my father; more instances of sexual abuse than I could remember; and the reality that my childhood had been filled with unsafe situations which inflicted years of pain long after I had left home. But I also had to acknowledge my own poor choices, the patterns of covering up and harboring wounds and pain. And then there were the years of giving permission to all the wrong people. I had to face them head-on. I had failed to create boundaries, became isolated in my thoughts, angry at others, and burned out in my work. I arrived at this place because I didn't see my pain through the right set of lenses. Instead of taking an honest look and processing my wounds, I nurtured, harbored, and recycled. I used it to withhold love, feelings of intimacy, kindness, honesty, and wholeness in my relationships. The truth is, I let my pain become my identity. It got there against my wishes, and I didn't start the process, so I felt self-righteous in carrying it around. My pain had a voice, it had a face, and it was powerful. My pain was me and I was my pain.

At some point in life, that pain is bigger than you can handle. It may seem to be stronger than you can harness or it's more haunting than your dreams can contain. Some factors add to it, like stress, lack of sleep, and the overwhelming numbers of people wanting more from you than should be reasonable.

The people you do life with need you to be complete. It would be wonderful if we wore little indicators pinned to our shirts that showed our individual capacity level. The badge could answer questions before someone interacts with us. They could alert others when we are overloaded by stress, capacity, demands, or altogether breaking. But those little meters don't exist, so we have to do something called self-care. That's when we keep our meters in good shape, and we know it. Beyond a day off or a bubble bath, we need to care enough to speak up for ourselves. Sure it's uncomfortable, but like anything, with practice comes ease.

You take your car in for oil, but they check the washer fluid, brake and transmission fluid, tire pressure, and a list of other factors influencing the ability for your car to perform at full power. Self-care happens when you check the heart, head, emotions, behaviors, pain level, and the repetitive breakdown experiences you have been having.

I would suggest that forgiveness might be a meter that should be checked with regularity. The cost of letting your car's engine run with too little oil is dangerous and so is too much oil. Too much self-care can be serious because it becomes the focus of life; it builds narcissism and self-importance. Take care not to make the focus all about your selfish acts.

Here are some questions you can ask to check your gauges for healthy living:

- Do I feel well physically?
- Am I getting enough sleep?
- Am I eating well?
- When was the last time I found joy?

- Am I spending time with people that increase the value of my future?
- Who has been given too much permission to demand my time, talent, or emotional energy?
- Are the choices I'm making wise?
- Am I repeating behaviors that I know I shouldn't?
- Am I making everything about myself or my demands?

The cost of living an emotionally healthy lifestyle means determining the value of that health. Is it worth it to invest in the future? Just as importantly, consider this question: What is the cost of ignoring the situation? What will happen if I neglect to invest in forgiveness, right here and right now? Are your scales in balance? Is your village supporting you? And who is the person in the mirror—do I like the way they look?

That chain holding you back, the backpack you're lugging around, that weight that is attached to your body—is it worth the cost to cut it loose? Forgiveness is the means to experiencing the future you want and deserve. Is it worth the work? Will you be able to maintain it?

There is a cost to every decision you make in life. It may not be financial but does have value. Is the value of healthy living and getting yourself in a better place worth the cost associated with the journey? You won't know until you see it in the rearview mirror, but I promise, it's worth every penny—figuratively speaking. Buy those sunglasses, take off the mask, and enjoy the view—you've been waiting a very long time to experience it.

15

the value of broken

"Everything is laid out for you. Your path is straight ahead of you. Sometimes it's invisible, but it's there. You may not know where it's going, but you have to follow that path. It's the path to the Creator. It's the only path there is."

—Chief Leon Shenandoah

STAINED GLASS IS a beautiful use of broken pieces assembled with lead. When an outside light source shines through, a beautiful image emerges from the various shapes and colors placed together. Your heart is like that glass, sculpted together from each of the broken pieces of the past and ready to allow beauty to be seen when it lights up. Your stained-glass heart (the next item in your box) may not be created yet, but when it is, it will be perfectly shaped and ready to love again. When you work through the process of letting go, a new heart emerges from the rubble. It's a beautiful thing.

Have you ever lost something significant? Are you willing to look for it until you've exhausted all options? There's no need to continue looking for something once it's found. In the past fourteen chapters we have introduced you to several lost things that now are found. So how is your heart doing? Do you feel like it's beginning to be uncovered? Are all the pieces there? It's not likely that reading a book has caused you to miraculously unveil all of the answers, not all of them are clear. We know for sure that *what* you have lost is worth looking for, and reassembling it is worth the work.

Worthless things are never stolen. Have you ever noticed that? Robbery only happens when something is of value. When you allow yourself to be put down, abused, stepped on, or taken advantage of, you feel robbed. Your value is diminished. Sometimes it doesn't feel like you have a choice—and sometimes you really don't. Regardless, when you have been robbed, victimization occurs. Just like the other scenarios we've discussed, living as the victim is no place to hang out, nor is it a place where better things come to fruition.

The wounds you have were acquired through very real circumstances. The perceptions you have woven through your heart have robbed you of possibility. Today is the day you decide if it is worth the cost. You can fixate on hurting the person who hurt you, dream of what you should have said, or how you should have responded, but that won't fix anything. Looking in the rearview mirror is no way to live life. Your value is in the future, not the past.

Consider the words of David in Psalm 61: "O God, listen to me! Hear my prayer! For wherever I am, though far away at the ends of the earth, I will cry to you for help. When my heart is faint and overwhelmed, lead me to the mighty, towering Rock of safety. For you are my refuge, a high tower where my enemies can never reach me. I shall live forever in your tabernacle; oh, to be safe beneath the shelter of your wings! For you have heard my vows, O God, to praise you every day, and you have given me the blessings you reserve for those who reverence your name" (TLB).

It's hard to gain the proper perspective when you are hurt. David felt faint and overwhelmed. He needed safety, and he knew God could hear his cry for help. He didn't wallow in each detail. He asked God for help, acknowledged that wrong was done, and announced his need for something very different to occur.

In order to truly accept the future as the goal, you must stop; resist the temptation to idealize what was taken from you or what you missed out on. Don't fixate on the possibilities of delivering wounds back to the one who wounded you. Returning the favor of pain to that individual will not provide you with the satisfaction you might wish for. It might feel good now, but even the opportunity to confront them won't fix things. The more heinous their crime, the more this is true. Your future is what matters, and it's time to focus forward and decide where your energy should be spent.

Every life has ups and downs, and people have bumps and bruises. Every moment you hold onto the pain and focus backward—you rob yourself of living in the moment. Rebuilding self-respect, repairing relationships, moving beyond trauma, and letting go of the past take energy. The key to finding the end of the journey is the phrase, "I forgive you." Those are your words to focus upon, and they are the words you will give to someone else, whether they deserve them or not. These words give you the power to heal. How do you know if someone is actually sincere in their apology to you? That's a great question!

A properly constructed apology has five elements:

1. Regret – genuine and complete.
2. Responsibility – acceptance of the blame for what occurred—regardless of anyone else's actions.
3. Repentance – a willingness to change future behavior.
4. Request – the moment they ask for forgiveness.
5. Restoration – the commitment to making it right. This may include repayment of something lost or stolen or payment for something like alimony or child support.

Your response is also a process:

1. Acknowledgment – of their apology.
2. Not allowing them to excuse away the situation.
3. Adding a new set of rules that will help keep this from happening again.
4. Acceptance of their restoration plan.
5. Announcing the words, "I accept your apology; I forgive you."

When you say the words, "I forgive you," you are cutting the chains that have bound you to your wounds. You are choosing to focus on the people involved rather than the pain. When you decide to move forward despite all you have endured, that in itself is the moment you will encounter the liberating freedom we first spoke of in chapter 1.

The moment you're desperate enough to find what you're feeling and release its potential energy, you convert an adverse reaction into a positive beginning. When you make the decision to invest in yourself, to take the journey despite the cost, and to forgive even when it doesn't make sense, though it's one of the most painful experiences you can walk through, it is quite possibly the greatest gift you can ever give yourself.

At that exact moment you take power away from the wound, remove its toxicity, and commit to never returning the favor of your woundedness to the wounder. You own the power and will experience something unexplainable. It doesn't even have a name, and it might even feel like a bit of nothingness because it's actually a physical, emotional, and spiritual experience that happens simultaneously.

What does it feel like? There is a collision of pain, hope, joy, regret, worry, fear, anguish, and letting go that simultaneously occurs within a split second. What emerges from the dust is inner peace. This peace leads to joy, to emotional healing, and then to new life and renewed energy.

During this experience you must intentionally lock your focus on new experiences. You must exercise forward thinking and press on toward what is yet to come. Ahead you will find amazing potential and incredible possibility.

You have to resist the rearview mirror; the views it offers are dangerous and distorted. They have the power to draw you back in and make you question your forward movement. Don't believe those lies. The best days of your life really are ahead. Remember that your memories are never as clear as the way things happened. Do not let them deceive you.

It is with great importance that I point out that forgiveness is a journey, and there are possible pitfalls inside the path. Nobody ever said you need to be foolish enough to forget your journey. That pain is yours to remember. It has challenged, given you purpose, and brought you to this place. Forgetting might allow you to repeat the scenario, and there's no way you want to go back there again. There is a difference between remembering and reliving them.

Your memories of the past matter. Believe it or not, they keep you from hurting others in the ways you have been hurt. They provide caution for the next cliff you drive along and help you advocate for others. Those memories remind you where you came from or what you have overcome, and they empower you to be a better version of yourself when they have been reframed correctly.

You've got questions racing through your mind. Who do I have to forgive? Why should I choose to confront? Is it really all you say it is? Because you, your future children, family, and the next generation that you will influence—they all win. When your energy moves you forward, it helps you focus on what matters and empowers you to achieve new things, so you win. The choice to forgive is the decision to move toward the finish line. Don't forget, it's a marathon, and you have to run the race—one step at a time.

My friend Jeremy once said, "Don't you wish there was a magic ray gun that would take it all away and just fix it?" I might be the first in line to buy such a gadget if it landed on the market. Unfortunately that is still only science fiction. Instead it takes work, commitment to the journey, and courage. But when the potential energy is turning into forward movement, the joy of the journey begins.

Once you start moving, don't give up! This is no time to quit! I began to feel things I had not felt in a long time in my own experience, and I have begun to experience tears, emotions, and happiness I had suppressed far too long. The people in my life had more value, and I realize I am more valuable to them. I am building more important relationships and fewer fringe relationships. And I have begun to look in the mirror and see myself more clearly.

The miracle of transformation you can experience is worth every bit of hard work you've put in! Don't miss it. Don't discount it. And don't wait to get started moving toward it. You can experience pain-free, guilt-free, manipulation-free, forgiveness-filled living. But *you* are in the driver's seat, and you have to push the gas pedal in order to move forward.

When unforgiveness has overstayed its welcome, it has a way of shouting hurtful words from the dark corners of your mind. They repeat the negative messages you have worked to put away by dragging them out into the open over and over again. That means that in this forgiveness journey, there needs to be a new set of rules—a new cycle of living, a new you.

One thing we've learned is that giving permission for people to overuse you, take advantage, or wound you repeatedly is hard to control, but it is possible. The new you must be vigilant, alert, and willing to stand protectively against new wounds. That looks different for each of us, but there are a few things in common.

1. *Choose Healthy Relationships* – Giving and taking, encouraging and being encouraged, loving and being loved, listening and being listened to. In short—balance.
2. *Address Pain* – Speaking to people who have hurt you is hard. It takes practice, but learning that caring for others and allowing them to care for you requires open communication. Talk with people, not about them.
3. *Calm Your Spirit*– The storms won't ever go away; they are a reality of life. In the middle of the storm, you have choices. How will you respond? Look for wisdom, opportunity, and grace as you decide. Stay calm and keep moving in the right direction.
4. *Give Permission* – You'll always have people who want a piece of your time, your energy, and

resources. Choose wisely and only give permission to those who are going to help your future. Don't get back in the loop of providing permission to consume your time or use you. The answer has to be "no" more often than ever before. And not "no" with strings, guilt, or shame attached. Say "no" because it's right and because you know it is the best decision.

5. *Write About It* – Journaling is therapeutic. Listening to uplifting music, writing inner thoughts, drawing, painting, and storytelling help you be heard and share emotions in new ways. Reframe your pain and ask for wise counsel. You are encouraged to write your whole story and then rewrite your plans for the future. Go for it and make it great! Don't stop journaling or finding creative outlets. There is something special about writing your thoughts. They are a gift to yourself and the best way to measure your growth.
6. *Recognize This New Process* – Stop for a moment and recalibrate your surroundings. You have grown as a person. You didn't get here accidentally. Purpose happens on purpose. It is filled with intention and planning. Progression is needed to

create change, and in you change has begun. You are beginning to see that things can and should be different. You have come to a place where you are receiving things you didn't deserve or which you couldn't imagine. But even more importantly, you have reached a place where you are giving away grace—even grace that is undeserved.

A few years ago I was introduced to the beauty of Kintsugi pottery. Broken pottery is repaired when a skilled craftsman takes each piece, places it together, and mends it with lacquer that has been infused with precious metal. The result is stunning works of art constructed from what was previously useless. What had once been valuable pottery had become broken, but now it is put back together and displays new character and beauty that were not present in its past form. The weaknesses become the strongest and most valuable points of the piece because they tell a story.

As you encounter the new you in the mirror, you'll notice the beautifully repaired framework that's created because of this habit of forgiveness holding you together. This is a time to smile and celebrate God's wholeness in your life. You will discover that you are on a new and better path than you used to be. You may need to make other changes as you begin to discover the person you've been hiding under all of that pain. You won't be a perfect masterpiece overnight, but you will begin seeing beautiful moments partnered with a sense of belonging, strength, understanding, and a feeling of empowerment. Inside your chest is a heart with a second chance to feel and with the ability to love others—even yourself.

Today is a brand-new day!

Journaling Opportunity

- How about you, are you like that pottery?
- What broken things do you need to ask God to protect you from? What safety can He provide for you?
- Have you been reconstructed as you have worked through the journey of letting go? When you let go, did you trust God to control the future?
- What questions have you encountered that are still unanswered?
- Who can help you find the answers you are looking for?
- What actions do you need to take right now?

16

construction

"Holding on is believing that there's only a past;
letting go is knowing there's a future."
—Daphne Rose Kingma

OUR TIME TOGETHER is nearly over, and you have assembled an entire toolbox for the next chapter of your life. But let's create one more device that will help you succeed. As I hand you the final item in the box, it is quite useful even though it is imaginary. It's a paintbrush. It's here so you can create a new and beautiful work of art that will replace your past version of life. You don't have to be a skilled artist; you can keep adding and adjusting the scene until you've gotten it just right. This paintbrush is able to color inside the lines perfectly and create new and beautiful masterpieces. It's much like God—when we put Him in control, we should be amazed at the beauty He brings to each new day.

A term we often use is "mending fences." Forgiveness is a way that we repair broken boundaries, betrayed emotions, and feelings of rejection. Some of us have lived with our pain so long that we have forgotten how to construct proper fences. We have to learn the difference between barricades that keep our hearts from being hurt and those that come with properly constructed permission-giving skills.

From this point forward you will have the opportunity to let others wound you again or not. You can do that and you can keep forgiving them. But there is another option. You can take the term "mended fences" and look at it from an entirely different perspective. When a farmer mends a fence that has been broken, he is keeping his relationship with the next property owner in a good place. It keeps his livestock from mixing with the next herd over, or out of a field of corn, or even the road. The fence isn't there to keep the neighbor from ever visiting, and it has a greater purpose. The two property owners will remain friends longer if they have a set of boundaries and both agree to maintain them.

You have the choice to repeat your forgiveness habits as you have always done. But after our journey together I hope you can work with the relationships you have, in a way that rulemaking helps you be better neighbors with your friends and family members.

The first choice allows you to become wounded often. This response will continue to allow pain. When someone comes along that you want to have a good relationship with, you have to self-assess and ask if you're ready. Before now you've practiced protecting yourself from emotion. Now you may be tempted to experience the pattern of pushing people away—even when you don't want to. I challenge you to set up rules and accountability to prevent this.

The second option means learning how rules can be best suited for every relationship you have. You might say, "I'm not going to work after 6:00 p.m. any longer." That's a relationship rule with your boss, coworkers, family, and yourself. It limits the ability they have to take small bits of time you never intended for them to have. You could make a rule, "The kids will be in bed by 8:30, so the adults have some quiet time to wind down each day." That gives you the destressing time you need to get your life in order at the end of each day. You no longer fight with the kids about when bedtime should be; 8:30 is the answer.

Remember that making these rules means you have to be committed to holding up to your side of the bargain. It will be hard at first, but you'll see how they free you from the expectations that others were allowed to violate. You don't have to be the person others walk all over.

Have you been waiting for someone to release you from that? Today—you have that permission to stand up and be strong. Being a victim has taught you that others can control you, but as of today that no longer needs to be part of your plan. Allow yourself to reframe the view by investing in the new you.

One of the most wonderful experiences in life is when a child has created an intentional piece of artwork for you. Just last week, a child drew a picture for me that said, "I love you," on it. I had given her some of my time, and in return she expressed "I love you" because I had helped her see that she had let others take advantage of her. How simple is that!

We all need someone to listen, give us hope, and build us up. Making friends with the right people will allow us to feel loved and to offer love in return. It's like each person who encourages you adds a brick to the fortress that protects your heart. We can choose to build that fortress on our own, but just like the Kintsugi, adding other minerals (people) strengthens the bond and gives the whole piece more value.

Our final assessment is not about a negative cycle of decision-making. It's about the way you plan to stay strong and keep your transformed life in order. In this space you're going to intentionally choose to be kind to yourself and give yourself the time and energy you need to be nurtured back to health. This is where you will no longer be exposed to the damaging results of your past. You need a way to keep robbers out, to keep potential energy in, and to feel safe, so you don't fall back into the practice of covering up what you don't like.

Imagine this tool like a structure. It could be a wall, fence, mote, or barricade. It's not there to make you feel calloused. It's there for you to use to keep yourself in good relationships with others. I love the concept of a bridge being offered to friends that want to visit. Regardless of your structure's shape, it has a defined place for foot traffic, and the shape of that space defines who and how people can access what is inside. This is the visual representation of your rules.

In many cases you can even close it off completely, depending on the situation. When people come to visit, you may choose to lower the structure or keep it up. You will have the power to decide. This boundary will protect your most tender emotions from future cycles of pain.

It is designed to be solid so you remember that safety matters. The world is a dangerous place and you need to be prepared for pitfalls.

While you're constructing, I want you to think about what you should bring inside the protected space. A few suggestions are your time, resources, yourself, identity, and the way you value your loved ones. Be cautious—letting the wrong people inside may cause you additional pain.

This boundary is to keep out trauma, abuse, and neglect. You can never remove the memories of what happened in the past, but you can bring the right resources along for the future.

This is a barrier. It is not intended to close people out, hide, or block your view of reality. You must build your fence with the future in mind. Protect the valuable version of you that is being created. The new you is fragile and needs extra protection as it emerges into the world. It's gaining in strength as it is being mended. And it won't take long for those wounds to be part of a story in the past.

Paint words like, "I love you," "You belong," "You are safe," "You deserve better," "Your life matters," or, "I'm sorry," on your structure. These words have the power to add strength to your resolve with the future, endurance, and shared protection. How much stronger might we be if others help us to find protection around our hearts? You've already defined those people in your life that can be invited to help you rebuild your protective boundaries. Invite them inside; share the view. Remember, many hands make work light, and those supporters will make this journey more enjoyable.

Having a protective space doesn't guarantee things will always be perfect. You should be wise to those who have robbed you in the past. You'll know that your fortifications are failing when you find yourself once again experiencing pain or resentment. You'll notice because you're staying home when you want to go out, and avoiding people who have offered help. You'll toy with putting on masks—believing that people can't see through them. Pain and resentment will appear like beacons screaming to the world and shouting out your fears. The noise will be loud, the temptation will be strong, and you may be blinded by untruth.

Those same patterns of doing absolutely anything to hide what is inside you will open up unwanted doorways and allow clouded judgment to come flooding inside. In moments when someone tries to address your fortress, you'll do ridiculous things to avoid reality and authenticity. That's why you have to be diligent to keep your structure safeguarded. This barrier reveals your forbidden features, unmasks your hidden rules, relieves you of unwelcome visitors, and illuminates the beauty of living. This structure is yours, and it matters more now than ever.

Forgiveness is funny—the more you give, the more you'll see that recalling details of the past is not as important as healing in the present. Let go of what you can't control. You've painted a new landscape, established a new foundation for life, and harnessed the power to transform your narrative. This is BIG! You built it; be proud of its workings. You designed it to guard your heart and to make sure future hunters, robbers, abusers, naysayers, and attackers don't have a chance to inflict the pain they intend to leave behind.

Journaling Opportunity

- If you could build a brand-new fence around your heart and unpack the dysfunctional bricks that got piled up to protect you from pain, what would that new fence look like?

- Is it possible that other people would have a key to the gate? Or maybe your gates could be left open for members of your village to pass through.
- Why do you need this new boundary? How will it keep you out of danger?
- Is the new fence around your heart joined with the fences of your village where you are now free to roam about peacefully?
- Are you expressing newfound emotions? Are you experiencing feelings you had forgotten?
- If not, what is holding you back? There's no better time to take the first step than right now.
- When you consider the word undeserved, are things beginning to rearrange in your mind? Are there undeserved moments you need to process differently?

17

the gift of freedom

*"Your level of forgiveness determines
your level of freedom."*
—Steven Furtick

TOES ARE YOUR most underrated body part! Yes, I said toes! You have ten of them, but do you really know why? One of the first milestones in life is when a baby finds their toes, but after that, few parents ever teach their kids about their importance.

Stubbed toes are a regular occurrence in my life, and no matter how many times I've already experienced the trauma, I'm amazed by how badly the pain can really hurt. A smashed toe can provide a variety of words at the moment and land you on your backside. And even worse is the experience of an ingrown toenail. For some reason we don't put a cast or splint on toes if they are broken, and for that reason I think toes often go ignored.

Or maybe it's because you have so many that you take them for granted.

I bet you've noticed when someone has nice-looking toenails or well-manicured feet. But that still doesn't make you focus on prioritizing your own foot care. Here's the thing; if you didn't have toes, you couldn't walk. Your toes keep your body connected to the ground while you walk. You run, dance, pivot, bounce, hop, skip, jump, and move in any specific direction because you have toes. They are quite powerful! Toes hold your entire body weight, add power to a well-directed ball, and administer pain to unsuspecting shins. You have ten toes for a reason—because you need them.

Similarly, God created you with another bodily function that you may discount—forgiveness. Sure, you don't have a physical appendage called forgiveness, but you have a need to keep that function of your body just as healthy as the rest. Simply stated, you can't do life without forgiveness. Take a moment to ponder that statement.

Along with the skills to exercise many different types of forgiveness, your daily decision-making process involves making the function of forgiveness stay in check.

Rule # 1: Forgiveness keeps you grounded, and without it, your emotional movement would be limited.

Rule #2: Dysfunctional forgiveness can add insult and further injury to limping functions.

Rule #3: You can't do life successfully without forgiveness!

Rule #4: When you offer forgiveness, you will find freedom for yourself.

Rule #5: Avoid procrastinating forgiveness. Don't quit before you are finished. And don't settle for halfway done.

When Peter asked Jesus how many times we should forgive others, Jesus replied, "Seven! Hardly. Try seventy times seven" (Matthew 18:22, MSG). You have so many opportunities to forgive. Imagine how much better you will be prepared to forgive if you have cared for the portion of you that has that ability.

As you move forward in this journey, you deserve a new beginning. You may believe your life is not worth redeeming, but it is. You may believe the person who wounded you is not worth forgiving, but they are. What work do you need to do in order to care for your forgiveness properly? By now you know who needs this action, and you have the tools to walk through the process. Every journey begins with the first step. And each journey can only happen one step at a time. They have to be your steps, and no one can walk them for you.

There's no magic formula called forgiveness, no perfectly slated recipe or step-by-step guide. It's a unique journey to every person in every situation, and it requires a commitment by you and only you. Upon delivering the gift, you will discover this type of collateral is worth everything you've risked making it happen. The precious value of your pain is notable, but it's still considerably less than the value of letting go. When you choose to give the gift of forgiveness, something unexplainable happens. It's life giving, and the life it gives is yours.

Six years ago I witnessed my abuser at the most difficult crossroad possible. After committing a horrific crime and completing a plan to take his own life, ventilators were supporting his comatose body, which lay still in a hospital bed. His life was on the line and doctors were fighting to save him. For some unknown reason God had mercifully given him an opportunity to keep living.

Something inside took over as I moved my entire schedule around; I altered every part of my life to help with his care. It was as if something empowered me to be the bigger person. This man was not the only one who had hurt me in horrific ways, but he was the main instigator of the grief in my life. Late one night I sat in the room reading Scripture to him, and I was overcome with the realization that this person had introduced me to incomprehensive drama and impaired living. Until then I compartmentalized him by using definitions like my perpetual wounder, my voice remover, the one who took so much from me. And at that moment I had the ability to remove the power of those debilitating voices.

It wasn't a split-second decision that landed me in the forgiveness mode. I questioned what would happen if I ignored the problem. I wondered if I had a responsibility to make it right—or if I was required to care more than I did. If I decided to forgive, would it be a one-time commitment, or would it be drawn out? To say I was lost was an understatement.

Emerging from the spinning wheels of thought, I found the resolve to make one of the most life-altering decisions ever. I doubt if anybody heard me, but I heard it. "I forgive you," bolted out of my mouth like a racehorse leaving the gate. Was it enough? Did I mean it? Were my motives genuine?

In an instant I had moved from victim to survivor, from survivor to a woman living free of thirty-year-old baggage he had loaded me down with. I offered the gift of forgiveness to someone in a moment when others would have chosen the opposite. What I received in return was ferociously stronger than I had imagined. The emotions spilled from my eyes, and instantaneous relief overwhelmed everything inside me. How could I have predicted this?

When I was younger my voice wasn't strong, and because of my inaction, others were severely hurt by his behavior. His unthinkable acts have crept into the corners of many lives. The most brutal round of the internal wrestling match was surprisingly quick.

Today we have a new set of rules. He doesn't have the same power to hurt me, he is not able to destroy my life, and I no longer give him permission to steal my joy. I gave the gift of forgiveness in a seemingly senseless moment, and I thought I was saying it for his benefit. If only I had known! Not only did it change my life to give it away, but he too has learned the power of the gift. Do I have regrets? You bet! Would I have done things differently if I had known how? Absolutely! But my choice to forgive has had ripple effects far more significant than myself.

My hope is that my unheard voice will somehow become your microphone. I confidently leave you with a new set of tools equipping you to give forgiveness away freely. The contents of this box will help you keep your balance, and I'm positive you can use these tools in ways you never imagined. I look in the rearview mirror, and I know that good things, great things, and healing things come after pain and suffering—and it's through those things that we grow.

In your life, there's a beautiful fence being constructed around a broken pot, and that pot is being masterfully rebuilt as we speak. Today you are at a crossroads. On the left you have a gift box equipped with useful tools, and on the right is the same path upon which you've entered. Which journey will you embark upon?

The beauty of this box is that it multiplies itself. The gift is not just a single box. When you most need them, you'll discover a whole stack of boxes with red ribbons waiting right here, ready for you to give away. The truth is, these symbols will show up in your daily life, and you will notice the visual connection they make as you consider the functional forgiveness concepts in this book.

A gift box filled with beauty, love, and God's promises includes reminders of things around you each day.

- A bandage
- A caution sign
- A "Do Not Enter" sign
- A fuzzy hamster on a wheel
- A heart
- A magnifying glass
- A microphone
- A paintbrush
- A pair of sunglasses
- A pebble in your shoe
- A photograph
- A scale
- A sheriff's badge
- A starting line
- A string

All wrapped up with a big red bow.

Each symbol provided points toward God's plan of forgiveness for you and me. And together they bring your memories to this place where healing begins. Who you were before we met does not define who you are today or who you will become—but it does influence how strong you will be when you get there.

Forgiveness is an intentional set of practices that allow God to bring you out of pain and into a relationship with Himself. Needless to say that's an ongoing process. Over time you will not just see it, feel it, and experience it; you will also begin to give it freely. You'll discover how to use it logically and get inspired as you share your experience with others. Forgiveness is a key to the most beautiful version of tomorrow you can imagine. The freedom you will experience is beyond comprehension. What's next will never be like what once was, and that, my friend, is a promise!

More Journaling Opportunities

- What is next for you?
- Make a list of newly significant words in your life.
- Journal about your experience. Why is letting go so powerful?

- What gift(s) have you received as you've packed up your baggage and replaced it with joy, peace, patience, love, and happiness?
- How have you changed your definition of significance?
- How has your relationship with your offender or perpetrator changed?
- How are you helping others and contributing to their well-being?
- How are you practicing being present with others?
- How are you passing the act of forgiveness-gifting to the next generation?
- What things are you doing to keep your fear/hate/anger/destruction under control?
- What new journeys do you need to embark upon to be the best version of yourself?
- Write your story—all of it. Don't forget to acknowledge the part where you started winning.

sources of stats on abusers

https://melmagazine.com/en-us/story/why-victims-abuse-become-abusers